ONLY THREE VOTES

The battle for the
political soul of Wales
Carmarthenshire 1967-74

Gwynoro Jones & Alun Gibbard

Without the following people, what happened to me during the period we are reviewing would not have come to pass.

I would therefore like to acknowledge the contributions of my former wife Laura, Ivor Morris the agent, and Gwyn Charles Carway, for their hard work, their enthusiasm and their untiring campaigning throughout the whole time. Also, the upbringing I had and the contribution of my family at my home in Manyrafon, Foelgastell, and the support of the many Labour Party workers in the Gwendraeth Valley and the hundreds across the constituency. Indeed, it was a great honour to represent the county of my birth in Westminster.

In addition, I would like to thank Janice Davies for the initial translation of the text of the Welsh version of this book. And Alun Gibbard for all his work in creating this biography.

ONLY THREE VOTES

The battle for the political soul of Wales
Carmarthenshire 1967-74

Gwynoro Jones & Alun Gibbard

Parthian, Cardigan SA43 1ED
www.parthianbooks.com
© Gwynoro Jones and Alun Gibbard
ISBN 978-1-917140-34-8
Cover design: www.theundercard.com
Edited by Dai Smith
Typeset by Elaine Sharples
Printed and bound by 4edge
Published with the financial support of the Welsh Books Council
The Modern Wales series receives support from the Rhys Davies Trust
A cataloguing record for this book is available from the British Library.

CONTENTS

I AM HERE WITH YOUR LABOUR CANDIDATE, MR GWYNORO JONES

I close my eyes to focus better, because this is now a long time ago.

It is 1967. I am twelve years old. It's Whitsun half term and the Urdd Eisteddfod is taking place in Carmarthen Park, three minutes' walk from home. My brother and I have already been with my mother to the opening Gymanfa Ganu, unnerved by being separated from her in that great crowd, because, in 1967, men and women, and even boys and girls, must be divided for harmonic purposes. It's also the last time I was to see tonic sol fa printed alongside the *emynau*, because, as I said, this is a long time ago, closer to the First World War and the only Welsh Prime Minister than we are to 1967 today.

I've come back to the Eisteddfod by myself in the week, on a hot early June day. I've borrowed an early simultaneous translation device from the BBC stand because, while I hear Welsh spoken every day, nobody at home ever speaks Welsh to me. Out of a device which looks like a large wooden spoon I can hear the voice of that great broadcaster, Alun Williams, and he is translating the speech being given by a man I can see on the stage a long way away and whom I know very well to be Gwynfor Evans.

Tall, white haired and faintly aristocratic, it is almost a year since his groundbreaking victory in the Carmarthen by-election. I'd spent nearly a year at Carmarthen Boys Grammar School where a collection of English-only road signs could be found dumped in the car-park in the morning, and where much older boys would come up to you in the playground, shake hands, and say in a solemn voice, 'Gwynfor'. Here he is, in every sense, in front of a home crowd. His platform speaking style is underwhelming, but what sticks in my memory the most is a passage where he tells his audience that:

'the rise of nationalism in Wales is like the tide beating on the shore.
And it's coming in.
It's coming in.
And it's coming in'.

And by the third iteration, the crowd in that hot and airless tent were on their collective feet, roaring their approval.

And I didn't like it, one bit.

Fast forward now to October 1974, seven years and, at that age, a lifetime later.

About half-way through that period I'd already made my mind up (and for a lifetime) that I was a socialist and not a nationalist.

For the first time, I was about to steel myself to be a foot soldier in the Labour army knocking doors to support my heroes in what remains the most talented Cabinet, yes, of my lifetime.

At 10 o'clock we've assembled at St John's car park. I am with Richard Edwards, then as now, a fellow socialist, and we are dispatched to spend the morning canvassing the good citizens of White Mill, just outside the town. Our small team is led by a lovely man, and lecturer in English at Trinity College, Don Dale Jones. He is, however, incorrigibly and (in the White Mill context) unfathomably English himself.

Neophyte door knockers in the Labour Party, at least, are generally advised to watch another more experienced practitioner, before having a go themselves. Don's example was to raise his deer stalker hat, as he marched towards the voter (always a 'housewife' at home in 1960s Carmarthenshire) and to say, in a voice which began loud and, deploying a crescendo which Rossini would have envied, ended in a boom which ran, 'Madam, I am canvassing you on behalf of the LABOUR PARTY'.

I'm not sure what effect it had on the voters, but at the age of nineteen it certainly terrified me.

For the afternoon session we were taken far away to the northern end of the constituency and the village of Cwmann, and a further addition to our crash course in canvassing. We were to be 'knockers up', calling voters to the doorstep and holding them there long enough to experience the magic of meeting the candidate.

Only, in this case, it really was magical. We'd been taken to meet the candidate, and the Member of Parliament with the smallest majority in the House of Commons in an equally small café before the session began. I thought I had never seen anyone who looked more exhausted. Gwynoro Jones, for it was he, was slumped over a cup of tea, looking every bit a man who believed that a majority of three was unlikely to see him home.

Until, that is, a voter came into view. At a distance of 50 yards, it was like a light came on inside Gwynoro. He straightened up, thrust out his hand and got ready to impress. And in 1960s Cwmann, he did just that. This was canvassing I could manage, and even enjoy. Voters (still housewives in the afternoon) would answer the door dressed in a pinny and slippers. I would say, in Welsh just good enough for the purpose, 'I am here with your Member of Parliament, Mr (note the 'Mr') Gwynoro Jones. He'd really like to meet you'. And with a cry of alarm, my interlocutor would disappear back into the house and reappear in shoes and something suitable for meeting a Member of Parliament in those deferential days. By then, Mr Jones himself had appeared on the doorstep, and I could move on to the next knocking up, before any awkward questions could be raised.

Gwynoro was, in many ways, the antithesis of the Gwynfor Evans I remembered from 1966. Short, where Gwynfor was tall; a young man, where Gwynfor was not, and very clearly more at home on a Carmarthenshire doorstep than I could imagine the more reserved, slightly aesthetic President of Plaid Cymru. Gwynoro's Welsh was the language of the chapel, not the text-book. It bubbled up and flowed out of him, as the hymn says, 'without ceasing'. Whatever his later political peregrinations (and I knew, even then, that someone who had served as a personal private secretary (PPS) to Roy Jenkins was hardly likely to belong to 'my' part of the Party) he was the embodiment, that day, of a message which I've remembered and tried to live up to, ever since – that in Wales, you don't have to be a nationalist to prove that you are Welsh.

In this book, then, you will find the vivid eyewitness account of one protagonist's participation in some of the most memorable events in recent Welsh history, told by a man whose understanding of their significance was, and is, both instinctive and persuasive – and told in a voice which draws the reader directly into the rhythms and the *teimlad* of the time.

But, you will also find much more than that. These were events which prefigured, and did much to shape the political battles of the last half century, the devolution half century in Wales. They shaped the non-nationalist, but distinctive Welsh social democratic preferences of the last sixty years. For anyone interested in the formative moments of today's Wales, this is both essential and highly entertaining reading.

Mark Drakeford
First Minister of Wales 2018-2024
Cardiff, Wales March 2024

ONLY THREE VOTES

"WHAT ARE YOU DOING FOR THE REST OF THE SUMMER, GWYNORO?"

Sometimes a career, or indeed the true course of life, can turn on the most sudden and insignificant events. That is certainly what happened to me. I'm going back to May 1967, a mere week before the famous *Summer of Love* in California. Perhaps indeed that event had a more global effect, but what happened to me that summer is key to the way that the rest of my career and my life developed.

On the day in question, I had a day off from my work as an assistant economist with the Gas Board. I had recently bought a house in Llanishen, Cardiff and I was about to get married to Laura Miles, a girl from Garnswllt, Ammanford. Life was good, and simple enough.

A school and university friend of mine, Arwel Davies, happened to be free, and so we decided to go down to Penarth for a walk.

As we walked along the prom, enjoying a chat and the sea air, a car pulled up beside us. I knew the driver well, it was Jack Evans, a Labour Party candidate in Carmarthen in the 1955 General Election. I didn't remember him from that electoral campaign, but I came to know about him, and to understand that he came within three thousand votes of Sir Rhys Hopkin Morris, a famous and distinguished Liberal, former Regional Director BBC Wales and Commons Deputy Speaker. Jennie Eirian was the Plaid Cymru candidate. Later, Jack became Megan Lloyd George's agent when she became a Member of Parliament in 1957, in a by-election following the death of Morris. It is interesting to note that Morris defeated the Labour Party by less than 500 votes in both the 1950 and 1951 elections. Close battles are part of the history of the Carmarthen constituency.

After some polite and friendly small talk, Jack asked me, "What are you doing for the rest of the summer?"

I told him that I was getting married that August. His answer came back, without taking any notice to what I had said.

"Have you considered venturing into the world of politics at all?"

Budding Politician

I had been interested in politics since I was a young boy. It was in the air in that part of the Gwendraeth Valley where I was brought up; the most westerly point of the South Wales Coalfield, mined for the hard coal – the anthracite – not the steam coal. This was the miners' radical cauldron, where politics was discussed on the coal face, in the shop and the pub. And such a place would, of course, be a stronghold of the Labour Party.

But more relevant to me personally, I went to Cardiff University in 1962 to study Economics, Government and International Relations. This is where I met Neil Kinnock for the first time, although the two of us never got on at all. There was an obvious distance between us, which would reveal itself in Westminster ten years later. I'm sure that both of us were at the complete opposite poles of the Labour movement in Wales. Barry Jones, the broadcaster and political correspondent, was also there at the time, as was Vincent Kane, the influential broadcaster. There was a political tint to college days.

Whilst I was in college, President John F Kennedy was assassinated. That caused shock waves throughout the world and was one of those popular political events that had an overreaching effect. I will never forget the Labour Party's response at the time, or at least, of one of the Party leaders; George Brown who was their spokesperson on foreign affairs, with Labour in opposition. He appeared on television to respond officially. He had had too much to drink and made a real mess of the interview, much to the embarrassment of the Labour Party.

During the summer holidays between 1962 and 1965, I worked first in the Carmel Quarry and then in Cynheidre colliery. This was real hard work, with workers whose education was mainly from the school of life but they were the salt of the earth. Working shoulder to shoulder with them was a priceless experience, regarding understanding the everyday life of the majority of the population. Another learning curve for me was being part of the "parliament" that happened every lunchtime in my father's carpenter's shed. This is where I first heard political, religious and general discussion and debating and there was also a lot of fun to be had.

My final year in university was the year of the 1964 General Election. I started becoming more active politically in my local area. I was assistant secretary of the Labour Party in Cefneithin, a member of the General Management Committee for Carmarthen Constituency, as well as a parish councillor in Llanarthne.

By the time I had the conversation with Jack Evans in

Penarth, I had already campaigned with him during the 1966 General Election and the famous by-election that followed. I had canvassed for the Labour Party candidate, Gwilym Prys Davies. Jack knew that I had an interest in politics. However I had just started an exciting new job in Cardiff as an assistant economist in Wales Gas Board, having been working in Dafen Llanelli with INA Needle Bearings for a year prior to that. I was happy professionally and personally. I was now living much closer to my fiancée, Laura, who was a student of Fine Art at Newport.

Carmarthen Constituency

When Megan Lloyd-George was first chosen as the Labour Party candidate for the 1957 election, she had only just left the Liberal Party. She won the nomination by just one vote. Her opponent was John Morris, who was at the time the deputy-secretary of the Farm Workers' Union of Wales in Carmarthen, but later went on to become the Member of Parliament for Aberavon for forty-two years in a career that included posts as the Secretary of State for Wales and the Solicitor General.

In the 1957 campaign Megan Lloyd-George defeated the Liberal party candidate by over 3,000 votes. In the three elections that followed she increased her majority each time, winning by over 9,000 votes in the General Election on 31 March 1966. At that election, due to her increasing ill-health, her nephew Benji Carey-Evans and Gwilym Prys Davies ran the Labour campaign.

But by 1966, it was an open secret amongst members of the Labour Party that Lady Megan was not well. In public, it was said that she had a virus, but a lot of individuals inside the party knew that she had cancer.

Anyone involved with the mechanism of the election in Carmarthen at the time were aware of the rumours that Lady Megan Lloyd-George was seriously ill. She shouldn't have stood in the election, and that was the opinion of many within her own party. I was an eighteen-year-old teenager at the time, and I knew the seriousness of Lady Megan's illness. But for some reason, Gwynfor's agent didn't know.

The problem was that nobody was prepared to tell Lady Megan this. No one was willing to take the responsibility of trying to persuade her not to stand even though they believed that she shouldn't do so. So, she carried on and stood as a candidate, visiting the constituency once during the three-week campaign, and won the seat. Nobody was too confident that she would continue as a Member of Parliament for very long after her resounding victory of more than 9,000 of a majority. And so it was. Lady Megan died from breast cancer on the 18th May, seven weeks after her victory in the General Election.

With better planning, more careful vision by the Labour Party, and perhaps more confidence to discuss the situation with Lady Megan herself, there would have been no need for that second election in 1966, which proved to be so historical for Plaid Cymru.

But a by-election was coming, and that's when I got involved. We had a new candidate in Gwilym Prys Davies. He came from north Wales, and at the time, was a solicitor in Pontypridd. I can see him now at the selection meeting making his speech with his hands visibly shaking as he held his notes.

There was another person being considered to stand for the Labour Party in the constituency, a young barrister from Cynwyl Elfed, by the name of Denzil Davies. He gave a confident and intelligent speech. But it was obvious that the whole mechanism of the Labour Party locally and in Wales, via Transport House in Cardiff, was behind Gwilym Prys Davies, and he was the 'chosen one' and inevitably selected. Even to me as a young twenty-four-year-old man and somewhat politically inexperienced, it was obvious that the wrong man had been chosen to stand for the Labour Party for the July 1966 by-election.

I went out to the highways and byways to campaign for Gwilym Prys Davies and often with the man himself. Whilst walking the streets of the Gwendraeth Valley, it became obvious that the voters didn't understand his north-Walian accent, while he didn't know the area or its people. On top of all this, despite being academically qualified and with significant experience within the party as an adviser on policy matters he was a man it was difficult to warm to. He was the complete opposite not only to Denzil Davies but in part to Gwynfor Evans also.

The country's economic situation was very difficult for Harold Wilson's incoming government. The pound was struggling on international markets. Jobs in the coal industry were disappearing. These were bullets for Gwynfor. It was a means for him to develop his tale regarding the relationship between Wales and London.

When the election day itself came, 14 July 1966, it was a disastrous day for the Labour Party. In the General Election, Gwynfor had been a poor third, he had made no progress since the 1964 election, which was quite a shock to everyone who knew him and probably to Gwynfor. At the by-election there was a lower turnout, with 4,454 fewer people actually voting, and yet Gwynfor won by a majority of 2,436. Plaid Cymru's share of the vote had increased from 7,000 to 16,000. Labour's former majority was shattered, and Plaid Cymru had their first member of parliament. Without a doubt, the political history of Carmarthen and the whole of Wales had changed completely.

Winning the by-election saved Gwynfor's future as his party's leader. Ever since the events surrounding Tryweryn and the disappointments of the Plaid Cymru's performances in the 64 and 66 elections there were many on the national committee who were highly critical of his leadership. These came from the left wing of the party who felt that Gwynfor failed to appreciate the economic and industrial problems facing Wales and was too prone to make pronouncements on cultural and linguistic issues. Foremost among them were D.J. Williams, Emrys Roberts and Harri Webb. These were significant figures within the party. DJ Williams was one of the founders of Plaid Cymru, Emrys Roberts, who until 1964 was general secretary of Plaid Cymru, and Harri Webb was an influential and outspoken poet and one-time editor of Plaid Cymru's magazine. Roberts argued that Gwynfor was "shy, weak, unimaginative and lacking in drive".

The political commentator and writer Dr Phil Williams was another figure sceptical of Gwynfor's leadership after the Carmarthen by-election. In a book focusing on the later elections in key south Wales constituencies Williams claimed that it was not the Carmarthen result that was the sensation but the party's performance in the Rhondda and Caerphilly by-election results.

Carmarthen was a Welsh-speaking rural constituency; Gwynfor had an enormous personal vote; it had never been a safe Labour seat... The Rhondda was an even larger swing to Plaid Cymru, was English speaking and industrial... the citadel of the Labour Party.

The reaction of the Labour Party faithful in the constituency was without doubt a devastating blow. They felt that the Labour Party had deceived them in allowing Lady Megan to fight the General Election, knowing that she didn't have long to live. Many felt they had lost faith in the Labour Party in the months prior to the first election in 1966 and certainly after that. If Denzil Davies had been chosen for the March election, which is what should have happened in my view, there would have been no need for a by-election in July, and Gwynfor would have remained a poor third – who knows?

But a question also arises as to how eager Denzil was to be a candidate in the first place. In a letter to John Morris from Trevor Griffiths, a very prominent member of the Labour Party in Carmarthen, he said that Denzil would be quite happy to be on the shortlist. A strong suggestion that it was not a burning ambition of his.

But not everybody thought that the Labour Party's situation was impossible. This is what Sir Ifan ap Owen Edwards said in a letter to Cledwyn Hughes, following the election in March 1966:

*Amongst the lessons I have learnt from this last election,
is the one that the Nationalist Party, under the current
circumstances, can never succeed as a political party
and that the Labour Party is now the National Party of
Wales. It would be wonderful if Gwynfor and one or two
similar to him could come to you to swell the ranks.*

Jack's Suggestion

That is the broader background to the meeting between
myself and a man that stopped at my side in his car in
Penarth. Through working with Jack Evans in the July
1966 election was the trigger for Jack to ask me to
consider being a candidate myself.

Of course, my activities in 1966 also placed me at the
centre of a historical event in Welsh political life. It
increased my awareness of Gwynfor Evans's story. I knew
about him because of the County Council, but I didn't
know much more than that.

There wasn't much connection between myself and
Plaid Cymru before the 1966 campaigning. I had some
knowledge of Gwynfor Evans from 1964 onwards, but I
had no interest in Plaid Cymru at all. I knew two or three
Plaid members in Cefneithin, and enjoyed debating with
them, either in their homes or at the side of the road. The
three were the bard, Dai Culpitt, Will Rees and Jac Davies,
one half of the famous singers Jac a Wil. When I was in
the secondary school, I spent many hours in Jac's house
discussing politics, even though we both had different
viewpoints.

Jack Evans was completely convinced that I was the one
to fight against Plaid Cymru in 1970.

"Many of us believe that you would be the best candidate."

"Why do you say that?"

"Well, there are several things in your favour. Firstly, you come from the Gwendraeth Valley, you're from mining and farming stock, you speak Welsh, you've graduated, and you have a young person's enthusiasm."

That is the exact reasoning that the Labour Party should have followed in 1966 when thinking about Denzil Davies or Gwilym Prys. They were a year or more behind, but at least they caught up! It was obvious that Jack had thought a lot about me before making his suggestion but after he said all this, as he sat in his car, he added something that was quite a shock to me.

"You won't win, of course; Gwynfor will be there for years."

I wasn't quite sure how to react to such a comment, so I didn't. Instead, I asked him what I should do next if I wanted to be a candidate. He explained the process, including writing up a letter to each ward in the constituency, and getting in touch with every Trade Union connected to the Party, every Labour Women's section, as well as visit a list of key individuals.

The seed had been planted. A leisurely visit to the seaside turned into a trigger to make me consider doing something that hadn't crossed my mind. My journey to the world of full-time politics had started.

STARTING THE BATTLE

It didn't take me long to decide to allow my name to be considered for being a Labour candidate in Carmarthen, in line with Jack Evans's wish.

At that time, my father John Ellis was a carpenter working at the Cynheidre colliery. He was an extrovert who enjoyed political discussion and debate. His workshop at the pit was referred to as the "Cynheidre parliament". I had observed this parliament in action while working at the colliery during my vacations from university. The debates were broad with councillors, miner's agents and even a few Tory supporters taking part.

My father suggested that I should meet a number of key people in the area including local councillors and union representatives. He arranged several of these meetings for me. My campaign to be chosen as a candidate was gaining steam. I wrote to every branch of the party, plus the Labour Womens' sections and trade union affiliate organisations seeking their nomination. Most of them would invite potential candidates to address them before deciding on who to nominate. I received a letter from Jack Evans in June 1967, saying that Gwilym Prys Davies and Denzil Davies had said that they didn't intend to stand in Carmarthen in 1970 and that the closing date for the nominations was the 9 October.

That was the beginning of a fervent period of canvassing by me. The first political speech I ever gave was in Llandybie near Ammanford on 6 July 1967. After that, there was no end of meetings; in Brynaman, Cwmllynfell, Pontiets, Carway, everywhere possible. One remains in the memory. The Rose and Crown in Rhosaman; at a crowded meeting on the 21 July, it became clear that there were strong feelings opposed to Plaid Cymru.

Laura and I got married on the 19 August 1967 in her home village of Garnswllt. Both of us were to an extent in the public eye from the outset.

Brynamman Carnival.

The Selection Meeting

I had succeeded in securing the support of ten Party branches in the constituency, ten unions and two of the women's groups. With this support confirmed, a good performance in the selection meeting was going to be enough for me to be successful.

When the day of the meeting came, there were three names on the short list: Dr Ambrose Lloyd, a forty-one-year-old family doctor from Lampeter, a member of Ceredigion County Council and the County Health Management Committee; Will Evans, a fifty-one-year-old district councillor in the Carway area for over ten years, who had been chairman on every council committee as well as secretary of the Miners' Union lodge in the Pentremawr colliery. I was the third and just twenty-four years old. There were sixty-two members present at the selection meeting. I didn't get to know exactly the number of votes cast, but at the end of the afternoon, I had the majority of votes, and I was chosen after the first round.

Following the observation I made earlier regarding the folly of allowing Lady Megan Lloyd George to fight the election in March 1967, the relevance of that to my personal situation has not avoided me. If things had turned out differently and perhaps how they should have, I would not have had the opportunity to become a parliamentary candidate for Carmarthen. The world of politics turns on things like that.

Therefore, at twenty-four years of age and completely inexperienced, I was the prospective Labour Party candidate for the next General Election. With the enthusiasm of the young, I decided to start campaigning immediately, and began a campaign that lasted three years, right up to the general election. The first quotation of mine in the newspaper following the announcement that I was the candidate for Carmarthen was this:

This is a seat that can definitely be won back, and given the energy, enthusiasm and will to do so, we will win this seat back for Labour. The battle is on from now on, without a doubt.

That was in the *Evening Post* on Monday, 30 October, and several other papers also, I'm sure. My youthful enthusiasm was obvious!

The *Carmarthen Times* choose a rather different way to mark the story. As well as the usual front-page articles, this paper decided on Friday, 3 November, to combine politics and sport. In the column *Talking Sport* under the heading *RFC MP,* they drew attention to the fact that two former players of Cefneithin Rugby Club were fighting in the same General Election. Myself, former Cefen flanker, for the Carmarthen constituency, and Carwyn James, former Cefen outside-half and soon to be British and Irish Lions coach was standing in the Llanelli constituency in 1970. This is how the story ends:

All connected with Cefneithin RFC wish them well. Who knows, the club might benefit quite a lot if one of them is elected and becomes Minister in charge of sport!

In the *Carmarthen Times* also, a comment was made by the journalist Clem Thomas. I was described by him as:

24-year-old home-grown Welsh-speaking whiz-kid with a degree in politics...

Clem was an interesting character. He had been a part of Lady Megan's team and a prominent member of the Labour Party in Carmarthen. But something happened in the middle of the 60s that caused him to leave the Labour Party and turn to Plaid Cymru. I believe it was to do with him losing his officer position within the party. In the 1966 Election, he was a fervent follower of Gwynfor Evans. I kept in close contact with him throughout my campaign in the years leading up to the 1970 election, and he wrote quite a bit about me. Though I doubt that I convinced him with my politics.

Plaid Cymru and Labour 1966 -1970

As I settled into my work as a candidate, I knew that I had a battle ahead of me. In the constituency itself, I needed to revive the dire lack of morale of a Labour Party that had just taken a beating in the 66 by-election. In the selection meeting, I said, "I'm convinced that I can win back this seat with energy, enthusiasm and the will to win!" That is what stimulated me to keep a promise I also made that night, which was to go out into the constituency to meet people every weekend up until the election. I kept my promise.

But these were also difficult days for the Labour Party outside Carmarthen. Earlier in 1967, the Party took quite a shaking in the Rhondda. In a by-election in the Rhondda West constituency at the beginning of the year, Plaid Cymru came close to gaining the seat from the Labour Party. For years prior to this, Labour, in their traditional heartland, had enjoyed comfortable majorities of regularly over twenty thousand. When Plaid Cymru came within 2467 votes of winning, it was a terrific shock.

17

A year later, there was another shock. In the Caerphilly by-election, Phil Williams, the Plaid Cymru candidate, came within 1874 votes of beating the Labour Party, who again had always enjoyed significant majorities in the area. It felt that Nationalism was on the rise.

The Labour Party therefore had three knocks on the trot: 66, 67, 68; Carmarthen, Rhondda West and Caerphilly. Three very different areas to each other but with the same message to the Labour Party – the party was on its knees. In his review of Andrew Edwards's book, *Labour's Crisis: Plaid Cymru, the Conservatives and the Decline of the Labour Party in North-west Wales 1960-1974*, this is how Dr Martin Wright, from Cardiff University, sums up the general situation at the time:

Plaid Cymru, while still managing to retain the energy of a protest movement, had, by the end of the decade, developed realistic political aims, a credible economic policy and a robust local organisation. Emerging figures such as Dafydd Wigley and Dafydd Elis Thomas represented a new realism... In some senses, the 1960s marked Plaid Cymru's coming of age as a political party. The work of its general secretary, Emrys Roberts, contributed to modernisation at a national (Welsh) level, while the emergence of the radical Cymdeithas yr Iaith Gymraeg (The Welsh Language Society) allowed Plaid to focus on less controversial and more politically inclusive issues than the Welsh language. At a local level – in contrast to the Labour Party – Plaid was vigorous. The party strengthened its branch structure, developed a more active social calendar and focused upon the recruit-

ment of the young, while the adoption nationally of a range of populist, socialistic policies allowed the party to challenge Labour on its own ideological ground. This is not to mention, of course, the impact of Gwynfor Evans' spectacular election victory at Carmarthen in 1966. Considered together, these developments suggested that by the end of the 1960s Plaid Cymru was breaking out of the culturally exclusive mould within which it had been confined since its foundation in the 1920s.

There was an uphill task ahead of us, especially as I was fighting in the one constituency of the three named where Plaid Cymru had won.

Starting the Battle

My first public comments came quite soon after my nomination. The first one, unsurprisingly, involved Gwynfor Evans. On 17 November, I responded to a comment made by him: "there are definite signs," said Gwynfor Evans, "that the next Parliament would include a significant number of nationalist Members of Parliament from Scotland and Wales." I couldn't see that this was at all likely, and I said so in several newspaper articles and public speeches after that. This is one sentence that sums up my attitude at the time:

... my personal belief was that the Welsh people need more control over their affairs and should have an Elected Council and greater decentralisation of authority.

Of course, what Gwynfor declared didn't happen. Over the years, I became familiar with the overstating and over-colouring pronouncements made by Gwynfor and Plaid Cymru. Often, it was like creating a world of make-believe, something similar to "fake news" in this day and age.

I shared my second public opinion when I drew the attention of the Carmarthen electorate to an article in the *Western Mail* published on 10 October, which said that Plaid Cymru was distributing their literature in the Welsh chapels in London. I had been a lay preacher since I was eighteen years of age, and I continued to be until I reached my forties. I, therefore, had a definite opinion on religion and politics, and of the relationship there should be between the two. To me, Plaid Cymru's actions in London's Welsh chapels was crossing the line. I will return again to the role of chapels, and the Independent denomination in particular on Carmarthen politics at that time.

Then on the 23rd of November, I made a comment on a matter of policy. Lord Robens, Chairman of the National Coal Board, had said that there was a need to reduce the number of collieries and miners in the South Wales Coalfield. Robens was Chairman of the NCB for ten years, and reducing the number of coal mines was a prominent feature of his decade at the helm. The decline of the coal industry had started long before the days of Margaret Thatcher. Interestingly at one time Robens was also a Labour cabinet minister.

In response to Robens' announcement, I said:

> ... *if that was the Coal Board's plan, then new industrial estates must be set up in the Amman, Gwendraeth and*

Dulais Valleys, as well as the outlying areas of Llanelli,
before closing the mines...

Internal Battles

But I didn't expect that the first big battle to come my way
would come from within my own party. It was a reflection
of the spirit of the time, the spirit that caused the
problems for the Labour Party between 66 and 68. A
heading in the *Carmarthen Times* says it simply –
Gwynoro's Broadside. The story was a speech I made in
Llandeilo on Friday, 1 December 1967, during a social
event, calling for an official Welsh Labour Party to be established, one that would be essentially independent of
the central Labour Party on policy. My comments caused
quite a stir to say the least. As well as significant attention
in the local papers; I was interviewed on the news
magazine programme *Heddiw* on the BBC. Here are
snippets of the speech I made in Llandeilo, starting with
a statement that sets the argument succinctly:

> *In accordance with my aim of voicing the claims of*
> *Wales within the Labour movement, I believe it is*
> *important that an official Welsh Labour Party was es-*
> *tablished.*

That's it, simply. I then went on to outline the value of
establishing such a thing under three headings. Firstly, establishing a Welsh Labour Party would enable the Labour
Movement to hold an Annual Conference where it would
be possible to discuss problems relevant to Wales.
Secondly, there would then be a way to pass policy

matters relating to Wales. Thirdly, this activity would promote socialism throughout Wales.

At the time, the Labour Party had a regional office in Wales which arranged an annual Welsh Rally. But for me, that wasn't enough by a long way. The country needed its own voice. I made sure that I emphasised that my comments did not suggest for a minute that I wanted to see any sort of split within UK labour and that unity was key. My aim was to ensure a strong and powerful Welsh voice in the Labour movement. At the same time, I was invited to a rally in Newtown with Harold Wilson. Newtown is where the Labour All-Wales rallies were usually held at the time along with King's Hall in Aberystwyth.

It was my contention that establishing a Welsh Labour Party would give the country a much stronger voice than Plaid Cymru could offer. This was because of the strength of the Labour vote, the party's tradition in Wales and, as a result, the predominance of Welsh Labour Members of Parliament in Westminster. It was the party most likely to form an alternative government to the Tories and had the best chance of securing Wales's interests. To me there was no hope of Plaid Cymru doing this. My view was encapsulated in this way:

> *Apart from the suicidal notion of having a Wales completely independent from the rest of Britain, Plaid Cymru can only influence from the outside, and their interests are too parochial.*

But I also had comments about the Labour Party. One journalist from the *Carmarthen Times* asked me if I was aware of the structure of the Labour Party in Wales at the time. This was my reply:

> *To be absolutely honest, I don't know, and I believe that very few people do. More should be done anyway to give Labour supporters in Wales a unified voice... Revising the system as well as the name is essential. We must look closely at the organisation, the officers and policy... At the moment, nobody knows what goes on in the Labour Party in Wales.*

I added:

> *The aims of the official Wales Labour Party would not be narrow nationalism, but it would aim at furthering the needs of Wales, remembering that Socialism involves far wider horizons. I believe that the vast majority of people in Wales are socialist and have their country's interest at heart. I again reiterate, nationhood is above politics.*

And then the response came. The editorial article in the *Carmarthen Times* was clear. Referring to the Prime Minister at the time, Harold Wilson, it said:

> *The statement he made last week is certainly not from the readings of King Harold. And it is more than likely to upset others who view the movement through rose-tinted spectacles... Is this not what Plaid Cymru are seeking? Is this not in keeping with the policy of Welsh Liberalism? A rose by any other name perhaps? The idea*

may sound fine, but Socialists generally will sink it without trace. They will want nothing to do with any scheme which even skims the surface of those already advanced by other political organisations.

There was definitely a fierce response within the Labour Party, certainly locally. The first to declare his disagreement with my comments was Emrys Jones, the Labour Party's Regional Council organiser in Wales. He said that he wasn't at all happy with what I had said. I explained that I didn't think that the Regional Council was enough and that there was a need to establish a Welsh Labour Party, a party that obviously represented the country's interests. It was a regional party, not a national party, as far as Wales was concerned. Wales's interests, as a nation, were very important to me and close to my heart.

I have often thought if it wasn't for that meeting at the side of the road in Penarth, which direction would my political career have taken? In my heart, I was a cultural nationalist and a patriot. But in those days, I didn't believe that the way to realise any nationalistic vision was through Plaid Cymru. Yes, Gwynfor became popular after 1966. But it was only a small percentage of the population of the whole of Wales that knew anything about him, and only a small percentage were influenced by him. There was more hope to fight Wales's cause through a party that was more numerous than Plaid Cymru and one that also had many more Members of Parliament. But there was also a problem both within and outside the Labour Party; a significant number of the party's members were against devolution and often against the language.

It was going to be an uphill struggle. This was especially true of the industrial areas in south-east Wales, where up to twenty Labour Members of Parliament were strongly opposed to devolution and to the Welsh language. The three most fierce in their opposition were Neil Kinnock, Roy Hughes and Leo Abse. The attitude in Swansea was also the same, with people like Alan Williams, and Donald Coleman in Neath.

In stating my position with regard to a possible Welsh Labour Party, I had dealt a double blow. Firstly, in judging the Labour Party and the way it was run in Wales. Secondly, making observations that could be construed as nationalistic at a time when Plaid Cymru and nationalism were on the up. Unfortunately, back then, it was much easier to create a situation where the pure Labour followers believed that I had been polluted by Plaid Cymru! So it was that I was called to Transport House in London to explain my comments. I'm sure that the Labour Party officers were afraid that I had been too much influenced of what happened in the Rhondda and in 1966 Carmarthen itself.

Was I being influenced by the wider political climate? Not at all. But it was obvious that there was a worry that I was following the same path as the man I was supposed to fight against in the next election. There was no official disciplining, no reprimand, only some quite nervous and suspicious questioning. My message was: wake up! We are the party of Wales! There was no need for Plaid Cymru. But, unfortunately, at the time, only some ten per cent of the Labour Party's members in Wales could see the situation in that way; people like Cledwyn Hughes,

Goronwy Roberts, John Morris, Elystan Morgan, Tom Ellis and Will Edwards were the prominent ones. The first two were very prominent in the battle for a Welsh Parliament in the fifties, along with S O Davies of Merthyr, who introduced a Parliament for Wales bill in 1955.

These you will note are all men. At this time in the late 60s very few women were councillors yet alone MPs.

Within the Labour party, very few women would be on executive committees but their role inside the party was crucial. In Carmarthen there were probably eight or more Womens' sections and they would participate actively in local branch meetings and indeed meet seperately when needed. The driving force behind local activities – social gatherings, coffee mornings, fund raising such as bring and buy events.

The only woman MP in Wales was Eirene White who later became Baroness White. She was Labour MP for East Flintshire and very influential in the UK party – was chair of the National Executive 1968-9 and a Minister in the Wilson governments 1964-70.

Through the Women's sections they had influence but rarely power. It would take another couple of generations for that to change.

In UK Parliament in 1970s there were only about thirty women MPs – a small number but yet some became household names – Margaret Thatcher, Shirley Williams, Betty Boothroyd (later Commons Speaker), Bernatte Devlin the Republican firebrand, Winifred Ewing and Margo MacDonald from the SNP.

My observations that caused some consternation came at the end of 1967, with me still only a parliamentary candidate with limited experience. But I was convinced that the changes I advocated were what were needed at the time, and I don't regret what I said in Llandeilo. It would be more than twenty years later that a Welsh Labour party was eventually established.

My comments were part of a wider argument over Wales and its status, an argument that was still ongoing when the General Election came in 1970. This is how the man that lost to Gwynfor in 66, Gwilym Prys Davies, summed up the electoral campaigning:

> ... *campaigning in the by-election had very little to do with traditional nationalist issues but instead was a battle between two different types of Welsh nationalism, one housed in the Labour Party and the other in Plaid Cymru.*

Plaid Cymru was very quiet on my comments about a stronger Welsh identity for the Labour Party.

I did not yield in my campaigning for reforming the Labour Party in Wales. In 1968, following the third blow to Welsh Labour, namely the Caerphilly by-election result, I wrote a letter to the Carmarthenshire newspapers asking for a specific response from the Labour Party to what happened there. Under the heading, "What Labour Must Do", I first responded to Plaid Cymru's efforts in the constituency, saying that if they couldn't succeed in winning Caerphilly when there were so many political and economic considerations in their favour that year, then they didn't have a hope of winning a General Election there. Then, I gave the Labour Party a word of advice. I called for a positive response from my party, rather than resting on our laurels in the belief that the voters would come back to us anyway.

> *... the Labour Party should implement the policy outlined in its Election Manifesto, that is, give control for health, agriculture and education in Wales to the Welsh Office. Alongside this, there is need for an Elected Council, thus ending the farce of numerous nominated committees. The Labour Party need not fear change, but rather provide the people of Wales with the ability to influence the system of government in relation to aspects of Welsh Affairs.*

The end of the article is more emotional in its appeal.

> *Hence as a Welshman within the Labour movement we must start a dialogue with our fellow countrymen – especially the younger generation, so that the appeal to emotional patriotism poured on them is countered or mixed with reason. What is needed is an open debate before it is too late – for Wales.*

I am a Welshman, and one who loves his country.

Interestingly that open debate is accelerating over the last few years of the 21st century. Now we have an Independent Commission that is about to report on the future governance of Wales.

VIET NAM, A RAILWAY AND THE OCCASIONAL BOMB

During the year of the Llandeilo speech, I hadn't met Gwynfor Evans at all. That wasn't to happen until later in 1968. But there was an exchange of arguments, and that started in earnest right at the beginning of that year.

I wrote a long article to the newspapers under the heading "Gwynfor and I are poles apart". I began the article by noting the successes of the Labour Party in Wales at the time. After doing so, I referred to Plaid Cymru. This is what was in the *Carmarthen Times* on 5 January 1968:

Recently letters have been directed at some of my latest comments in the press, and reference has been made to the fact that Plaid Cymru is not anti-Labour, but it seems peculiar to me that people are able to state this and yet feel unable to give public praise to the Labour Government's achievements in Wales.

I then listed examples of how Wales had benefited because of the Labour Party. I highlighted the grants that came to Wales, the improvement in the hospital provision, and the establishment of the Welsh Office with a Secretary of State for Wales, both significant advances in the story of devolution. After saying this, I turned back to Plaid Cymru.

Finally, an article appeared in the Carmarthen Times, stating that Gwynfor Evans and myself appear to be almost on the same wavelength. May I state that this inferred that both of us want the best for Wales and for Carmarthenshire, then the reference is correct. But Plaid Cymru and I are poles apart on the best way to achieve this.

To have complete political separation, which would have economic consequences, is not the best way of attaining a better Wales. Those who do call for a Free Wales should have a look at the hard realities of economic life.

It placed clear water between Gwynfor and myself.

With this article in mind, it is interesting to note comments I heard from Elystan Morgan, the former Plaid Cymru parliamentary candidate who had been close to Gwynfor but who had joined the Labour Party, won the seat of Ceredigion and later served in Wilson's government. Elystan's had asked Gwynfor, "Is there anything that the Labour Party has done for Wales?" And each time, the answer that came back was "Nothing at all."

March 1968 was the first time I met Jim Griffiths, Member of Parliament for Llanelli and the first Secretary of State for Wales. He had just announced his intention not to stand in the next election. A celebration night was arranged at the Smiths Arms, Foelgastell to acknowledge his contribution to Welsh politics for half a century and more. At the time, Britain's economic situation was particularly hard, and as a young twenty-five-year-old man, I wanted to make my contribution to the cause. At that first meeting, I ventured to say to him, "These are difficult times, Jim." His reply said much about his experience in the years of the locusts in the 1920s and then during the war years: "Gwynoro bach, I remember difficult years!"

In the same meeting, Jim Griffiths said:

In the by-election, Gwynfor Evans won by gathering the protest vote against the difficulties which beset us. His vote was made up of a majority of electors who, whilst registering their protest, do not support the policies of Plaid Cymru. Labour will overcome these difficulties. This will compel Plaid Cymru to fight the next election on its own programme, which it has, so far, sought to cover up.

It is worth noting that in that same meeting, Jim Griffiths said that he hoped an elected Council for Wales would be established.

Meeting the secretary of state for Wales, Jim Griffiths.

Viet Nam

Gwynfor joined a group of people who were campaigning
for peace, against the war in Viet Nam. Amongst those
with him was the Welshman Emrys Hughes, a left-wing
Labour Party Member of Parliament in one of the Scottish
constituencies.

Since 1955, North and South Viet Nam had been at
war, and to complicate the situation, civil war existed
between groups within both countries. The United States
intervention in the war was the main objection to what
was happening there, and this was an objection that was
almost worldwide. Gwynfor felt that he wanted to show
Wales's support to those that were suffering in the war,
the people under oppression. Gwynfor was a pacifist and
a member of Heddychwyr Cymru, an organisation affili-
ated to the Peace Pledge Union and he had been a pacifist
and conscientious objector during World War II.

Plaid Cymru weren't unanimous in their support of
Gwynfor's intention to visit the country. Some, naturally
enough, were worried about his safety, and, indeed, his
life. On an ideological level, a more right-wing section of
the Party believed the visit would be interpreted as
support of the communist faction that was fighting against
the United States. Another worry, which was relevant to
me in the Carmarthen constituency, was that a foreign
visit of this type would reinforce the image which many
believed that Gwynfor gave of himself, which was as the
Member for Wales rather than the Member of Parliament
for the Carmarthen constituency.

But despite strong opposition from both within and
outside his Party, Gwynfor wasn't giving in and went on

his journey. He joined a group of twenty-five peace campaigners led by the civil rights activist Pat Arrowsmith and
including the seventy-two-year-old quaker Peggy Smith.
On the 3 January, Gwynfor flew to Phnom Penh, the
capital of Cambodia,with the group. Their intention was
to obtain visas there to go on to Viet Nam. But for
Gwynfor, Phnom Penn was not a step on the journey but
its end. He didn't have permission to go to Viet Nam. The
group was refused visas to both South and North Viet
Nam. Even so, his supporters back home were holding
prayer meetings to pray for his safety in a country at war.

On a more political level, this was an opportunity for
me to challenge his position. After returning from
Cambodia, Gwynfor spoke quite a lot about the situation
in Viet Nam, including several times in the House of
Commons. Two of his comments stimulated me to
respond in the press. Firstly, his suggestion that the
United States was to blame for the war in Viet Nam is the
statement he made during one parliamentary session in
Westminster. Secondly, he compared Plaid Cymru with the
National Liberation Front in South Viet Nam.

On the first point, some months before Gwynfor tried
to go to Viet Nam, I wrote an article outlining my response
to the situation there. In a letter to the editor at the
Carmarthen Journal at the beginning of December 1967,
I responded to a letter I received from someone in the constituency asking me about the war in Viet Nam. I started
by saying that I was strongly against what was happening
in that part of the world and that millions of innocent
people were suffering and being killed needlessly. I
predicted that neither side would win and that any talk

of victory was empty talk. I was also critical of America's intervention in the war.

America has lost the aim stated by the late President Kennedy when he said in 1963, "In the final analysis, it is their war."

I condemned the United States for the bombing of Viet Nam. But the essence of my letter to the *Carmarthen Journal* was that there was fault on both sides. In extending the argument to talk about other countries that were supporting different aspects of the war, I said:

But having expressed my opposition to the war and a condemnation of the extension of its execution to the bombing of north Vietnamese cities, let me hasten to add that both sides are at fault. Let those people who march and demonstrate outside the Russian and Chinese Embassies, both of which supply North Vietnam with weapons and technical aid for the continuation of the war... It is useful to remember that in December 1965, the Americans stopped bombing for thirty-six days in the hope there would be some response from North Vietnam, but this never materialised.

Gwynfor's journey to Asia annoyed many people. After he returned from Cambodia, he received an official reprimand from Plaid Cymru's Regional Committee in Carmarthen. In the same reprimand, another concern was raised. It was a concern to Plaid Cymru that Gwynfor travelled out of his constituency too often. He was asked not to do so as much in the months leading up to the election. The worry was that Gwynfor, as Plaid's only Member of Parliament, took delight in being referred to by many in his party as the 'Member for Wales' and not only Carmarthen. I am sure that was how Gwynfor saw himself. His attitude was more of someone who wanted to rule a country rather than just represent his constituency.

His voting record in the House of Commons was terrible. During his first term as MP there were nine hundred and ninety-five different voting sessions. Hansard records that Gwynfor voted in one hundred and fifty-five of them. In the course of researching this book, I have noticed, through looking at Hansard, that I voted more times in my first year in parliament than Gwynfor did in his whole time there between 1966-1970.

Bombs

Further clashes between Gwynfor and myself were over the use of violence in the name of defending principles and advancing the cause of a 'Free Wales'. The story began at the end of the previous year, 1967, some weeks after I was chosen as a candidate. A bomb was placed in the Temple of Peace in Cardiff, and the blast caused quite a bit of damage. Apparently, the bomb had been placed there to show opposition to a meeting which was to be held in the Temple to discuss arrangements for the Investiture of Prince Charles in 1969. Gwynfor was asked to condemn the use of violence in the name of nationalism. He refused to do so. He was also asked to do this on the floor of the House of Commons. He refused. This wasn't a surprise to me. Because immediately after winning the by-election, he said in the *Times*:

The government does not think anyone is serious until people blow up things or shoot others.

My response in the local press was to note that perhaps someone had taken Gwynfor Evans at his word.

In the *Western Mail* and on the television programme *Heddiw*, Gwynfor claimed that the bombing was the work of the Secret Services to bring shame and discredit to the nationalist cause.

There are other examples of this way of thinking. Elystan Morgan recalled an event that happened when he was a minister in the Home Office, when a man was found drowned in Foulness, on a piece of land owned by the Ministry of Defence in Shoeburyness. He was responsible for meeting boats that came to the shore to offload drugs. Gwynfor accused the Home Office and its secret agents of being responsible for the man's death. When the body was found, there was £500 in his pocket. According to the Home Office, the death was related to buying and selling drugs. Gwynfor accused Elystan of being involved in concealing the event.

Plaid Cymru distributed hundreds of leaflets in Ceredigion, Elystan's constituency, blaming him for being part of the plot. I know from my close friendship with Elystan in the last few years of his life that he was quite upset over Gwynfor's accusation and insinuation. Elystan would often tell me about what happened and I know very well that this innuendo disappointed Elystan greatly, especially the issue of distributing leaflets in his own constituency. After all, Gwynfor and Elystan were good friends for a long time when they were both part of Plaid Cymru. At that time withn the party, the expectation was that Elystan would succeed Gwynfor. His upset was rooted in his long-held admiration and genuine affection for Gwynfor.

The point was raised again in May 1968 when another bomb exploded in Cardiff, the fourth in the capital in a period of twelve months. I had to respond. Under the heading *Produce evidence or withdraw allegations*, in a newspaper article, I said:

> *To seriously suggest that the government finances secret agents to blow up its own offices in order to do the maximum damage to Plaid Cymru is irresponsible behaviour from a public figure... only a month ago, in a speech in Trimsaran, I warned the Nationalist party of the atmosphere they have helped to create in Wales where extremism and stronger action could materialise. Their choice of words on many occasions and their appeal to emotional patriotism has unfortunately been taken as an exhortation to action by certain elements in Wales.*

I was surprised that Plaid Cymru's only concern, after the bombing, was the political damage it had on them, and them alone. They weren't thinking about anyone except themselves.

> *They should have been aware in the first place of the damage, not to a party but to a nation; a smear on the character of a great and proud nation.*

After the bombing of the Temple of Peace at the end of 1967, Mr Cledwyn Hughes, the Secretary of State for Wales at the time, also referred to Gwynfor's comments on the secret service. In a statement from the Welsh Office, he said:

Mr Evans and other members of his party have been making increasingly wild statements, but this is the worst of them all. That it is entirely unfounded is shown by the prosecution that followed earlier explosions.

After the fourth incident of letting off bombs in Wales, the matter was discussed in the House of Commons. By May 1968, George Thomas was the Secretary of State for Wales, and he opened the debate in Parliament on 27 May. After he had reported the facts of the two latest incidents, namely the explosion at the Crown Buildings in Cathays Park in the centre of Cardiff on 25 May and the finding of a bomb in Lake Vyrnwy on the morning of the debate in Parliament, he made his political points, as Hansard shows:

It is clear that these outrages have been committed for political reasons. The House and the people of Wales will roundly condemn this attempt at political terrorism.

Two Welsh Members of Parliament, Emlyn Hooson of the Liberal Party and Ted Rowlands from the Labour Party, expressed their concerns that the efforts being made to find who was responsible for the bombs were not enough, whilst emphasising that such action was totally unacceptable to the majority of people in Wales. This is George Thomas's reply:

I do not know whether the honourable and learned Gentleman expects my right honourable Friend, the Prime Minister, to act as Sherlock Holmes [Laughter.] It is patently absurd to try to criticise the government because the police have not found the criminals. Unfortunately, on the last occasion when a man was found guilty and sentenced to twelve months imprisonment, the honourable Member for Carmarthen (Mr Gwynfor Evans) issued leaflets outside the court in which he said: "Although we do not agree with the action they have taken, we cannot condemn them." Any statement that encourages people to political violence is to be deplored.

Gwynfor was in Parliament that day, and he responded:

Is the minister aware that Plaid Cymru has condemned without reservation these outrages? [HON. MEMBERS: "Oh."] It has done so consistently. Is he aware that it condemns his own verbal explosion over the weekend, in which he said that Plaid Cymru had wrought havoc in the life of Wales? Will he withdraw that and apologise? Is he prepared to face the fact that the havoc has been in the Labour Party in Wales?

George Thomas said:

The honourable gentleman must have forgotten the leaflets he distributed at the time of the Tryweryn explosion. The leaflet he issued whilst the case was being tried said that those who blew up the transformer "... have merely tried to implement the wishes of the people of Wales..." I believe that statements of that sort have led to these bomb outrages.

Across this period, I often questioned Gwynfor's stance on the bombing, as well as his attitude towards the people who were behind any violent action. Without a doubt, his unwillingness to condemn the bombings weakened his image in Wales and particularly in the constituency. Had he stood more solidly, he would have strengthened his viewpoint and his standing. Throughout the constituency, there was still a strong echo of what he said after writing in *The Times* in 1966. They asked him then about his attitude, and his reply was weak. He had made a cross for himself very early on.

Taking a stance against direct action through violence nurtured additional relevance in the constituency and the county in general, as the residents experienced victory without using any form of violence some years earlier. The residents of Llangyndeyrn and district succeeded in over-turning plans to drown the area in order to create a reservoir. Following a long battle by the residents, the plans were abandoned, and the Llyn Briane dam near Llandovery was opened instead of in Llangyndeyrn. Jim Griffiths and Lady Megan also did much hard work in this campaign. Therefore, the effectiveness of non-violent action across the parties was alive and obvious to the people of the county.

It must be admitted that Gwynfor was in a very difficult

situation. On the one hand, there was the father figure Saunders Lewis, and others within Plaid Cymru, like Richard Wynne, saying that forcible actions were part of the nationalistic battle. He was the spokesman for Plaid Cymru matters in north Wales. On one television programme Richard Wynne claimed:

History has proved that constitutional methods alone is not enough.

It was difficult for Gwynfor to condemn those within his own party who supported such action.

That was my response to what happened at the time. The whole debate went on for several years. It is easy not to appreciate the effect of the debate regarding setting bombs in Wales in the Sixties.

After 1968 came to an end, I wrote an article in January 1969 looking back over the previous year, and that specifically in the context of the debate on bombing. Under the title "Plaid and the Bombs", I referred to a comment made by Plaid Cymru in the press. They were referring to George Thomas's reaction to the bombing and saying that his comments were "...*causing grave concern*..." to them. I didn't understand Plaid Cymru's response at all, even though it was obvious that they had changed their viewpoint on the matter during the year.

I find it extremely difficult to understand how the Nationalist Party can take a holier than thou attitude. While it is encouraging to see that the Nationalists are at last eager to lower the political temperature regarding bomb outrages, there are many questions and points one would like to highlight.

Yes, in the end, Plaid Cymru condemned the bombing and started to distance themselves from more extreme nationalistic actions. But there were still questions to be answered. Why had it taken so long for Plaid to make these comments?

An instance of this was the reported interview in The Times national newspaper in July 1966, by the President of the Nationalist Party, Mr Gwynfor Evans – the day after the Carmarthen by-election. In this interview, Mr Evans was asked if he thought the extremists would stop their activities since he had won Carmarthen.

Surely, here was an instance for Mr Evans to express his view on bomb outrages. But no! The answer was, "It is up to the government". Mr Evans then went on to state that "the government does not think anyone is serious until people blow up things or shoot others..." Maybe someone has taken these words literally?

Also, in the article, I drew attention to comments made by Richard Wynne suggesting that history showed that constitutional methods alone were not sufficient to create change. When asked if he would plant a bomb for Wales, his answer was "I would have to pull up my socks and do something..."

I ask is Mr Wynne still a member of the Nationalist party whose leaders speak a different language on the extremist issue?

I continued with the same point, but this time I turned my attention to nobody less than Saunders Lewis. He had just written an article in the magazine *Barn* saying a stance that depended on constitutional methods alone was "an unreal, childish and discourteous dream."

> *Surely, if the Nationalist Party leader's words are to mean anything, such an utterance, even though it came from the founding father of their movement, merits the question whether Mr Lewis is also still a member of the Nationalist party?*

My first year of campaigning was quite a lively one and at times unreasonably fierce. That fierceness came to the fore in the regular letters that appeared in the local newspapers between members of both parties. However, some of the letters were more like essays. That was the forum for political debate in those days, as my newspaper cuttings show quite clearly.

That year, Gwynfor had left the door ajar for me to be able to condemn him because of the irresponsible comments he made. That was my first impression of him as a politician, and they were far from being good impressions.

Personal Suggestions and Observations

I wrote to George Thomas, the Secretary of State for Wales, to suggest how the Labour Party should deal with Plaid Cymru. My impressions were, to an extent, based on what I had seen with Gwynfor in my first year of campaigning. In a memo to the Welsh Office, I said that there was a need for the Labour Party to take advantage of the turbulent climate that Plaid Cymru were creating. The title of the memo was "Suggestions". I wanted George Thomas to consider three specific points:

13. *The continual emphasis of the Nationalists on the "London" or "English" Government does create the wrong atmosphere. Such emotive words do not help.*
14. *Use of statements like "freeing" Wales also lends itself to various interpretations. Especially the words used by Gwynfor Evans after he returned from Cambodia – comparing the National Liberation Front of South Viet Nam to Plaid Cymru "fighting" for self-government.*
15. *Emphasise that in the early Sixties there was a definite silence from the Nationalist leaders regarding condemning bomb outrages.*

Rhys Evans's analysis of this, in his biography of Gwynfor, published by Y Lolfa in 2008, is interesting.

This caused significant damage to Plaid Cymru, and there is no doubt that the success of Welsh nationalism between 1966 and 1970 would have been that much greater if it wasn't for George Thomas and his continuous insinuations that Plaid Cymru was somehow responsible for the bombings.

But Gwynfor went much further in his attack on me. Rhys Evans's excellent biography of him identified a comment Gwynfor made about me. I quote from Rhys Evans's book:

... Gwynfor made the glaring mistake of taking Gwynoro lightly. This is how he described him to his friend Ioan Bowen Rees. He's completely self-confident, and painfully "big" and self-important (25 years of age): a clever tub-thumper. Therefore, the best way to treat him is to get people to laugh at him.

That was turning things personal. He also acted on his own suggestion at every possible opportunity. For example, he suggested to Ioan Bowen Rees that he should write a letter to the press to make fun of me. Also, Gwynfor himself wrote a letter to the press criticising me and identifying language errors as an example of my lack of ability, also identifying stories that included what he considered unintentional humour. This whole attitude of Gwynfor's was unhealthy, especially as he wrote the letter to the press under someone else's name.

He went further still. He made sure that one specific story was spread as widely as possible. I had been a lay preacher since the early Sixties; according to Gwynfor, when I was preaching, at the beginning of the sermon, I would declare from the pulpit that I was Gwynoro Jones and that I had an Economics degree. I only did that once. In the Methodist chapel in Llangadog. I was obviously invited to preach there long before I was chosen as a candidate. After that happened, the chapel deacons were unable to withdraw the invitation. When the secretary stood to make the announcements, he didn't name me or welcome me at all. It was a serious discourtesy and against the usual procedure.

When the collection ended, and I stood on my feet to

deliver my sermon I did say my name – because the secretary hadn't done so. I then gave a précis of who I was. That is the only time I did such a thing, and there was a specific reason for doing so. The fact that Gwynfor turned that story to his own political use was disappointing. It says a lot about the way he was prepared to operate.

In his book, *For the Sake of the Nation,* he refers to a period after he had surgery in a hospital in Middlesex, just before the 1970 election, and commented:

> *Gwynoro confidently forecast that I had only 6 months to live.*

I never said such a thing. I would never make such a comment about anyone. There was plenty of talk in the constituency about the fact that Gwynfor wasn't well, but that was the beginning and end of the comments. In fact I specifically told the executive committee members never to engage in or repeat any gossip about Gwynfor's health because I knew how Plaid people would go to the press about it should any member of the Labour Party be caught spreading the rumour.

Face-to-Face for the First Time

Early in 1968, the rail closures were a very hot topic. Plans were announced to close, amongst others, the railway which ran through mid-Wales. A deputation was arranged to visit the Welsh Office to discuss how the plans to close the railways were going to affect Carmarthenshire and the remainder of west Wales. The deputation consisted of representatives from the local authorities, railway unions and railway users as well as Jim Griffiths, the Member of Parliament for Llanelli, Elystan Morgan and the maverick MP for Pembroke Desmond Donnelly. They were there to meet with the Secretary of State, Mr Cledwyn Hughes. But Gwynfor, as Member of Parliament for Carmarthen, wasn't there. The question had to be asked, where was he? What was more important than the future of the railway in his own constituency? The answer? Lunch with the Foreign Press Association in the Dorchester Hotel in London. Before the day of the meeting, Gwynfor had made a number of comments about cuts to the railways in Wales. But his priorities were obviously quite different on the day. He had presented me with another golden opportunity to make my point in the press and in various meetings.

These were two more matters, together with devaluing the pound, which contributed to the difficulties the Labour Party now faced as the 1970 General Election loomed. But, instead of taking advantage of that, Gwynfor again made one of his superficial and irresponsible statements. He said that if the railroad between Carmarthen and Aberystwyth closed, then that would be the end of Carmarthen station. It was a silly overstatement. It was obvious he had forgotten that Carmarthen station was central to the service between London and west Wales.

This issue brought Gwynfor's personality to the forefront. It was as though he was completely unaware, bordering on oblivious, of any potential negative and critical comments his actions resulted in.

Following the meeting in the Welsh Office, the first opportunity came for me to meet Gwynfor face-to-face. I hadn't met him at all until April 1968. The National Union of Railway Workers had arranged a meeting under the title "Save the Central Wales Line". Several hundred people came together in Llandovery on a Saturday morning. There was an intention to close the town's station. It was clear from the beginning that the meeting wasn't a party-political one. There was a wide span of speakers present from several parties and organisations. I had prepared a speech for the meeting on that basis. The focus was the closing of a railway and a station and the effect of that on communities. That was the most important consideration for everyone.

I was sharing the same stage with Gwynfor and a number of other speakers. But his approach to the meeting was different to everybody else's. For him it was another opportunity to score party political points and not to deal with the subject of the meeting. I could tell the audience was frustrated. He started his speech by fiercely attacking the Labour Party and Mr Harold Wilson, the Prime Minister. "It is obvious", he said, "as far as the Labour Party was concerned, Wales was a peninsula that could be ignored, and its future is to be nothing more than a playing field for people from England". I was incensed by such an attitude and the specific comments made by him. I stood up and held my copy of the speech I was to give that morning high in the air above my head. I said that I had prepared a speech that wasn't one with party political tones. But following Gwynfor Evans's aggressive and wholly partisan approach, I would respond in kind. So, I tore my speech in two in front of everyone. I made a speech without notes, attacking Gwynfor, who was sitting next to me. If Gwynfor truly believed that I was someone who was superficial and to be taken lightly, I think he realised that morning that it was going to be the complete opposite.

Labour Leaders in My Square Mile

In May 1968, the opportunity arose to welcome one of the Labour Party leaders to the Gwendraeth Valley. There were more than two hundred people in the hall at Ysgol Maes yr Yrfa in the village of Cefneithin to hear George Thomas, the Secretary of State for Wales, giving his first speech since taking office. It was also the first time I had ever met him. From that day on, meetings between us became more regular. He would for example, come to my grandmother's and my parents' home for coffee. The root of our collaboration was our opposition to Plaid Cymru's nationalism; perhaps we were coming to that from different directions, but it was a battle that united us. That was one of his greatest attributes – until you come face-to-face with the real George. But more about that later.

It was at this meeting at Maes yr Yrfa that George Thomas first used the term "best friend Wales ever had" when speaking about Harold Wilson, the Prime Minister. It was a good phrase and one that was very beneficial to use in the Carmarthen constituency. The second thing I remember from that meeting was his emphasis that the awareness of the nation was something that overcomes politics. "There was a new generation of Members of Parliament", he said, "who were just as patriotic towards Wales as any nationalist".

I used this occasion to repeat my comments on the need to establish a Welsh Labour Party and to call for devolving more power from Westminster to the Welsh Office, in particular,.farming and health. Jim Griffiths had also made similar comments that year.

It's hard to believe, less than a year after the Maes yr Yrfa meeting, that the topics of a Welsh Labour Party and extending devolution were going to be the subject of fierce and bitter debate between George Thomas and myself.

Two Meetings

There were two other occasions when Gwynfor provided opportunities for me to challenge and criticise him. It is hard to believe that more than once, he failed to appear in key meetings in his constituency. Here are two examples.

A public meeting was called to object to the closing of the coal mines and to call for the opening of new industrial units in Ammanford if the mines had to close. In a meeting in that town, the Secretary of State was present, along with representatives of the miners and the Coal Board, Denzil Davies and myself, amongst a number of others. But Gwynfor wasn't there. This was difficult to accept in light of his constant accusations against the Labour party on this subject, but yet again, when there was a need for all to unite in confronting the challenge ahead he was nowhere to be seen.

The second meeting was in County Hall, Carmarthen. George Thomas again was there, and the intention was to lobby him to speed up the process of building new roads in the county. This was another issue that Gwynfor had made a lot of noise about. But he wasn't in the meeting. He said that he had to chair a session at Plaid Cymru's conference in Aberystwyth. For me it was an open goal.

> *... there was an excellent opportunity to leave the Secretary of State in no doubt as to the feelings of Carmarthenshire people... Far too often we have experienced that the constituency MP has his priorities completely out of line.*

I suggested that he could leave Aberystwyth for a few hours in order to be in his constituency for such an important meeting. When Gwynfor heard about my comments, the answer came back:

> *On the question of roads, I have made it a national issue in Wales. I have said so much about the issue that I have earned myself the nickname, "Gwynfor Dual Carriageway".*

It would be more correct to say it was not a nickname that he had earned but more one that he and his loyal followers had created.

Looking Back

In another newspaper article in January 1969, once again I looked back over the year. But this time I assessed the influence of the Labour Party on political campaigning that year. It was clear that I believed a very significant change had happened in the constituency.

Last year witnessed in the Carmarthen constituency the

period when people no longer took the emotional appeal of nationalism as any answer for all Wales's problems.

In 1968, I believed that the Labour Party had succeeded in reviving its position and once again was contributing to the political life of the constituency. That was extremely heartening. But I also realised that there was still a need to face a great number of problems. Onwards to 1969.

CROESO 69

1969 started quietly; but on the first day of the year, a campaign started that would gain increasing significance as the year moved on. Cymdeithas yr Iaith started painting road signs. It was a battle that would divide not only the Welsh and non-Welsh but also created divisions within the Welsh-speaking communities. The bombing had already done this, and it would continue to do so. Thus in 69 another avenue of division arose which caused further polarisation.

At the beginning of the year, I made speeches and wrote articles for newspapers on matters I believed were central to the Carmarthen constituency. This was the period I first used the term "Druids of Despair" to describe people who were all too ready to denounce Wales and to be completely negative about its economic situation. The worst Druids of Despair were the ones who were motivated by party politics. It seems to me that there are still such people around in the Senedd, but now they belong to the Conservative party more so than Plaid Cymru.

I am sure that the people of the Principality are fed up with the politically motivated opportunists who are not prepared to concede that the government has done more for Wales than any previous administration.

That, simply, was how it was for me. Wales had more from Wilson's government by the end of the sixties than it has had from any previous administration. Furthermore, a succession of cabinet members would visit Wales regularly. Over a period of seven years, 1969 until 1974, I became quite close to Harold Wilson. He came to Carmarthen three times. I'm sure that the beginning of this relationship followed a report I had prepared on the Carmarthen constituency.

I decided that it would be a positive and beneficial action for me to undertake detailed research into the economic, health, transport infrastructure and farming situation, and other significant matters, in the Carmarthen constituency. I prepared a twelve-page report in an attempt to pull a number of various factors together, many of which had a direct effect on the constituency's wealth. The first section discussed the area's economic situation and identified four main problems that faced the constituency, namely the road network, new jobs, farming and tourism.

It was obvious that there was a need to improve the roads throughout the whole of Carmarthenshire. This was a topic where Gwynfor created a name for himself, the infamous *Gwynfor Dual Carriageway*. It's a wonder that members of Plaid Cymru continue to use that name. It is one part of the myth that has grown around Gwynfor. I don't believe that he studied the facts about roads in the county or made a detailed assessment of what was needed – even though he was the Member of Parliament. Certainly, he hadn't costed the work that was needed to alleviate the traffic, especially in Carmarthen town itself. Gwynfor saw an opportunity to take a cause where others had done the work, so that he could keep some hold on constituency matters, instead of his main priority, namely being the Member for Wales.

In August 1969, for example, I sent a memorandum to George Thomas, as Secretary of State for Wales, outlining a clear plan to deal with the traffic problem in Carmarthen. At that time, it could take well over an hour to go through the town, a real pain for local people and for tourists on their way down west. The traffic queues on the A48 and the A40 when trying to get past Carmarthen towards the west were several miles long on weekends, especially in the summer time. In my report, I outlined a ten-year plan, that would cost £30 million. The suggestions included by-passes for Carmarthen, Pontarddulais, St Clears, Llandeilo, Llandovery and Ammanford. Later that month, following a visit to Carmarthen by Harold Wilson, the government announced that a temporary Bailey bridge would be built across the river in the town as an interim measure to alleviate the problem. It was to be a second crossing of the Towy river.

My report offered suggestions on what work was needed on which roads in the constituency as well as the cost. I also discussed the need to attract new industry into the area, following the continued decline of the coal industry and while at it suggested raising small factory units in several places. With regard to farming, the situation was dire. In an article in the *Carmarthen Times* in February 1969, after I had finished the report, I said this:

Coming from an agricultural background with many relatives closely connected with farming I am becoming increasingly aware of the fact that agricultural policy will be one of the most important issues of the next election.

And in discussing the effect of Plaid Cymru's nationalism on farming, this is how I saw it:

I recently cited the case of the milk transport costs problem as an excellent example as to why Wales should not be independent from England. Welsh farmers are able to object vigorously to the claims of south-east England, but a separate English government would automatically give preference to the south-east.

Of course, roads, farming, new industry and tourism were all tied together. More and more people had to travel further to work from the rural areas. More and more were visiting the county. Better roads were needed and more local work and better provision for the new tourism that was coming to the area. I presented the report, which discussed all these issues, to Harold Wilson. I am completely sure that the Member of Parliament for Carmarthen at the time hadn't done anything like that report. That wasn't the nature of his relationship with his constituency.

Callaghan and the First Baby

One morning in March, I was sitting at my desk on the seventh floor of Snelling House building in Cardiff, when I received an unexpected call to see T. Mervyn Jones, the chairman of Wales Gas whose office was on the ninth floor. People at my level in the organisation didn't get calls like that, and there were all sorts of questions going around in my head as I climbed the stairs up to his office. There was more of a shock waiting for me when I arrived.

Mervyn Jones told me that he had received a telephone call from Jim Callaghan, the Member of Parliament for Cardiff South-east, and the Home Secretary in Harold Wilson's cabinet at the time. He had asked Wales Gas if they would release me from my post so that I could become the Research and Public Relations Officer for the Labour Party in Wales. More than that, Callaghan also asked for assurance from Mervyn Jones that should I lose in the 1970 General Election that I would have my old job back. Mervyn Jones agreed to the request and the condition. That took me entirely by surprise.

I left Wales Gas and started work a couple of hundred yards away in Charles Street. It was, in one way, a step on a path I pursued after being chosen as a candidate, namely emphasising the need to create a Welsh Labour Party. At least now, I had responsibility over one clear aspect of the Party's work throughout Wales.

During this time, Laura was also expecting our first child. With the baby due any minute, any day, I was called to meet with George Thomas in Gwydir House in London. There was a great deal of discussion as to whether I should go or not, but Laura was happy for me to go. I walked into George's office and before I sat down, the phone rang. George answered and turned to me, "You'd better go home, Gwynoro!"

The train journey from London to Cardiff took some five hours in the late 1960s. I just about got home in time to be with Laura but it was not an easy birth and it took quite a long time for the baby, a boy, to be born, in Glossop maternity hospital Cardiff. Our first child was named Glyndwr Cennydd. There really was a change in my life that month.

It was a time when I had to fully immerse myself in working in the constituency, and that went hand in hand with my new family responsibilities. I was both delighted with my first child but also continued enthusiastically with my work in the constituency. Others noticed that activity. Gwyn Charles, President of the Constituency Labour Party, commented on my canvassing work.

Indeed, never can I recall a candidate in this constituency in the last twenty years being so prepared to go out and meet the people. The response to this energetic young man has been very favourable.

The first decision I took as Research and Public Relations officer for the party in Wales was to visit the executive committee of the Labour party in each constituency across industrial south Wales. The Party, to be honest, had sat on its backside for far too long. When I turned up at every executive meeting, without exception, I would be lucky if there was half a dozen there, when there should have been close to thirty. It was an eye-opener and a great disappointment to me. It was easy to lose heart. The Labour Party had a big problem. Many of the membership had become either lethargic or disillusioned and often seemed uncaring. The Members of Parliament as a cohort were largely edging towards retirement age except very few were preparing to step down. It had become a tradition to soldier on and die in office. And they were almost always men. It became obvious that there was a major task to raise the image and increase activity to promote the Party. Reform was needed.

The Party's literature and promotional material was practically non-existent. I set about changing all that. Part of that process was to visit George Thomas every fortnight to gather information from him for the creation of articles and leaflets etc. I created a list of two hundred people in the thirty-six constituencies who could, when needed, write to the newspapers on a wide range of subjects. There was no identifiable eagerness on the part of the Party at that time to do any public work in the name of promoting itself or in attracting new members. I suppose the view had been that there was no need for them to do too much with thirty out of the thirty-six seats in Wales in the hands of the Labour Party. Complacency ruled.

My work was to radically alter the situation to ensure that it wasn't apathy that carried the day. I think the leaders of the Party had noticed that I had done such work in my own constituency, so they believed I could extend that activity throughout Wales. I certainly did that and we started to produce a quarterly paper under the name *The Radical*. We also produced a four-page broadsheet for each constituency, something we take for granted these days.

A further boost to my confidence came when the Liberal Party announced their candidate for Carmarthen at the next election would be Huw Thomas. Thomas was a familiar name throughout Britain as he was the main news presenter for Independent Television News at the time. In his first speech as a candidate, with some three hundred people in attendance, he attacked Plaid Cymru fiercely and Gwynfor Evans specifically:

How dare this man say that he speaks for Wales, how dare he speak on behalf of all Welsh people.

It was the beginning of a fierce battle between Huw Thomas and Gwynfor. I wasn't going to be the only one to confront Gwynfor. The following was one of Huw Thomas's other attacks:

Who do these people think they are? You get the same symptoms wherever you have nationalism. You have only got to look back to Nazi Germany to see the same sort of thing. The Nazis were arrogant and intolerant of everybody... Violence is to be seen in Wales at the moment and the violence we are experiencing is going to get worse. These violent people are Welsh Nationalists. They are not Liberals, Tories or Socialists.

After such attention, Gwynfor changed his usual practice of letting others answer for him. He answered Huw Thomas directly. This was music to Huw's ears. Under the heading "Slanging Match Continues", the *Carmarthen Times* published a letter from Huw Thomas.

I am encouraged that my first attack on the Nationalists should have caused Mr Gwynfor Evans to break his usual practice of "not replying in the press to vulgar abuse by opponents". It must surely mean that those of my points reported in the press must have been true, and the truth hurts; otherwise why did he not leave it to the intelligence and experience of Carmarthenshire people to determine whether I was "violent and extreme" or whether in fact what I said was worth saying.

Indeed, it has brought forth another spate of his usual arrogant misstatements, and I will not allow a foreigner – a Barry man – to hoodwink my fellow county men and women.

From my point of view, there was now someone else making the same type of stand against Gwynfor, his policies and pretentious attitude.

He says the only people who put loyalty to Wales first are those who choose to live in Wales. Where do I start to deal with this further example of arrogance?

Very few Welshmen, including myself, would choose to live in a grim industrial city like London. Even Mr Evans was heard to remark recently that he much prefers to spend his time in Carmarthenshire. Who can blame him for saying this? Nearly every Welshman, wherever he has had to find a job outside Wales, would willingly change lots with Mr Gwynfor Evans. A wonderfully big modern house with a lovely view of the Towy Valley and a prosperous, pleasant market gardening business. If all Welshmen would have been in a position to do this – what heddwch!

Without a doubt, Huw Thomas's comments hit the nail on the head. To be perfectly honest, I know from experience and verbal evidence that that was the attitude of many villagers in Llangadog, especially the people who worked for him and lived on the council estate in the village. Time after time, on the doorstep when canvassing, I heard people complaining about the way they were treated and paid. I had no direct evidence of that, but I heard it regularly over the years of campaigning. One of the councillors for the area would come to me relatively often in order to share the complaints he was receiving from people who worked in the business. From what I remember, he was asking my advice on one central point which arose from what the workers were saying to him, namely that there was no union for the workers in Gwynfor's business. As a result, they couldn't complain about anything.

I felt uncomfortable raising the matter in public in case people accuse me of playing politics with a personal matter. I didn't know anything about Gwynfor's business until I read Rhys Evans's biography of 2008. There I learnt of the quite serious financial difficulties Gwynfor's business had been facing. He was confronted with having to close the business, and it was only the financial intervention of his brother Alcwyn that stopped this from happening. The biography states that one clear factor in the fervent efforts to try and save the business was the fuss that would be made by the Labour Party and the other parties because of Gwynfor's difficulties.

At that time, there was a less tolerant understanding of bankruptcy or even just business failure, and as a result, there would be significant political points to be scored by Gwynfor's opponents had his business failed. Gwynfor was very fortunate that his business problems didn't surface in the press at the time. I would have made use of the information in my campaigning.

In the fervent discussions that were taking place amongst members of Gwynfor's family throughout the period of the financial difficulties, there is one letter to him from his sister Ceridwen that shows how unhappy she was with the poor state of the workplace.

> *I really cannot understand Gwynfor why all these wonderful opportunities in such a glorious part of Wales are left to rot... If English people bought the farm and glasshouses and made an attractive estate of it, I suppose it would get bashed about.*

It was quite possible that Gwynfor was unable to pay his workers properly, and not that he was unwilling to do so.

In time I came to realise why, when it came to the 1970 election and canvassing was taking place, the vast majority of houses in the Llangadog council estate had my posters in their windows. After looking further into the reason for my support in Gwynfor's own village, the dissatisfaction with Gwynfor, the employer, was a constant complaint. I understand that it's very easy to complain about your boss, but the number that actually did so, suggests more than that. From the outside it seemed when I entered the council house estate, I was stepping into some kind of master and tenant environment.

When Huw Thomas was claiming that Gwynfor favoured remaining at home in Carmarthenshire, I understood only too well what that meant. Although he was the

Member of Parliament for Carmarthen, his voting record in the House of Commons did not show an MP committed to the democratic process. His main contribution was written questions. You could do those from anywhere – and in Gwynfor's case usually, back home in Carmarthen. Huw Thomas had also noticed Gwynfor's arrogant attitude. But Gwynfor has attracted a lot of votes from the Liberals in the 66 by-election. This, and his dislike of nationalism, was a strong motivation in Thomas campaigning with some vigour to win those voters back to the Liberal cause.

Wil Edwards, the young MP for Meirionydd, in a speech in Llandeilo referred to Gwynfor as "...the ageing Bernadette..." which was a reference to the young political campaigner in Ireland, Bernadette Devlin, and one who sympathised with the aims of the IRA.

Denzil Davies also criticized Gwynfor. Gwynfor was a figure of deep distrust for the Labour party.

I wrote in a letter that suggested Gwynfor was very good at leading nationalistic protestors to the prison door but then leaving them there and going back to the comfort of his home.

Charles and Devolution

As 1969 drew to an end, one of the major issues of my campaign was devolution. I called on the government to devolve health and farming to Wales. That was the first step in my campaign for calling for an Elected Council or Assembly for Wales thirty years before that actually happened. There had been a nominated Council for Wales and Monmouthshire established in 1948 later to be followed by a Welsh Council but there had been very little support or interest in either. In 1957 the Welsh Council set out the case for the office of Secretary of State for Wales and a Welsh Office. The Labour government of 1964 brought it all to fruition. However a handful of Labour Members of Parliament were making the case for an Elected Council as often advocated by Jim Griffith and others. Prominent in that campaign were Cledwyn Hughes, Elystan Morgan, John Morris, S.O. Davies and Goronwy Roberts.

From my perspective the devolution debate turned much more serious when I was asked to chair a working party for the Labour Party in Wales to prepare the party's evidence to the Crowther Commission on devolution. After Crowther died during the process, it became the Kilbrandon Commission. We were a team of ten; in their midst the lecturer and broadcaster Barry Jones, Bruce George, a farmer from Monmouthshire, and later a Labour Member of Parliament, Wyn Thomas, who later became famous through the *Swansea Sound* radio station, and Gareth Howell, the son of Lyn Howell of the Welsh Tourist Board. I also believe that Paul Flynn and Alun Michael contributed to several reports of the working group.

Within the British Labour Party, there was ample discussion and suggestions on matters relating to the Commission. In June 1968, John Morris, a minister in the Transport Ministry, wrote a letter to Harold Wilson stating clearly that he was in favour of devolution and an elected assembly for Wales. Then in August 1969, George Thomas also wrote to Wilson, creating the impression that he favoured devolution but at best he was agnostic about it.

All he was doing in his letter was listing a number of suggestions that were likely to be in the Labour Party in Wales's evidence to the Crowther/Kilbrandon Commission.

I was meeting George every fortnight at his home on King George V Drive in Cardiff, and he was therefore receiving full information on the team's discussions on every matter. Palpably it was incorrect and misleading, as Gwynfor and Plaid Cymru were forever saying that the Labour Party were doing nothing about devolution.

There is no doubt that the biggest event of that year was the Investiture of Prince Charles as the Prince of Wales at Caernarfon Castle. The event caused controversy in Wales as the preparations went ahead. It was the focus of the United Kingdom and the rest of the world on the 1 July, the day of the investiture. There were four thousand guests present at the castle. It was estimated that nineteen million watched it on television in the UK and five hundred million around the world. Debates over the need for a Prince of Wales and the investiture carried on for months following the event as politicians evaluated the implications the investiture had on Wales. It was the political issue of the year.

THE INVESTITURE

It's strange to say that one of the features of the period leading up to the Investiture, in the Carmarthen constituency at least, was the lack of attention in the local newspapers. In a period of enthusiastic political letter writing, there were hardly any letters on what was happening to Prince Charles in Wales that year. There was plenty of talk at the roadside throughout all the villages. The event was popular although there was a minority who objected to the ceremony, notably elements within Plaid Cymru and republican supporters.

The timing of the Investiture was beneficial to the Labour government. Indeed some were of the view that it was designed to deflect the Welsh people from more serious issues. Earlier I mentioned how the party in Wales had been shaken to its core. Plaid Cymru won Carmarthen in 1966 and had achieved substantial gains in Caerphilly and Rhondda West. Labour knew it needed to fight back. It considered that giving approval to the Investiture would be a popular and acceptable step by the people of Wales, who were willing enough to accept Charles.

It became obvious that Plaid Cymru were divided on the whole matter. The new young talented men, Dafydd Elis Thomas, the Leader of Young Plaid Cymru at the time, and Dafydd Wigley, were strongly against the Investiture and made their stand in public. In an article in the *Western Mail* at the time, it is said that those two, together with Dafydd Iwan and his songs, had greatly influenced the minority who were against the Investiture, including Cymdeithas yr Iaith of course. I must emphasise that the Party didn't officially support the Investiture. In 1968 Plaid Cymru decided that they wouldn't be forming a policy on the matter. But many of their members were supportive enough.

In *Gwaedd yng Nghymru*, a collection of articles by the philosopher J.R. Jones, we have an analysis of the political climate at the end of the Sixties. He was one of the early supporters of Cymdeithas yr Iaith:

> *To justify staying out of the protest, Plaid Cymru argues that a vesting ceremony is irrelevant to its campaign to gain independence for Wales; a "free Wales" would not recognise the sovereignty of the crown. To persuade Cymdeithas yr Iaith not to interfere in the protest, a slightly different argument is used, namely that the Investiture is not relevant to the Cymdeithas' field of protesting activities, as its official name shows, that is the Welsh language.*

The collection of articles is extremely interesting, and they talk about the new attitude towards Welshness that was developing in the period. Clearly, many different definitions exist and saying that there is only one type is an over-simplification. J.R. Jones has his own clear opinion, but in developing it, he comments on the different comprehension of Welshness that existed in Wales at the time. It was far from being black and white.

According to an opinion poll in the *Western Mail* at the time and referenced by Hansard 70% of the people of

Wales were very willing to welcome the Investiture ceremony to Caernarfon and to welcome Prince Charles as Prince of Wales. This would have included a significant number of Welsh speakers and Plaid Cymru supporters. Wales of course is never a straightforward country. Gwynfor's opinions and statements were supported by influential figures from within his own party, but this cohort were really a small minority in the whole of Wales.

Plaid Cymru's lack of support for the Investiture had, without a doubt, disappointed many people. But what made things much worse was Gwynfor's decision not to attend the ceremony himself. There was an invitation for every Welsh Member of Parliament to be present. Many in his constituency weren't happy with the fact that their Member of Parliament would not be representing them in a ceremony that was so popular.

There was to be more salt in the wound, and it was Gwynfor himself who put the salt there. Although he was on a rare visit to Westminster on the day of the Investiture, he made sure that he would be back in his constituency to meet the new Prince of Wales on his journey to Carmarthen. That was one of the biggest mistakes of Gwynfor's political life. People had come to accept that he wouldn't be in the ceremony, but they were not ready to accept that he was ready to meet with the prince when he arrived in Carmarthen on his itinerary around Wales after the Investiture. Many nationalists had said that they would stand against Plaid Cymru in the election if Gwynfor met Prince Charles. They felt that strongly. To the majority meeting the prince was pure hypocrisy. As a result, Gwynfor lost a lot of respect. Had he stuck to his belief, the outcome could have been different for him. Even some of his fellow nationalists called him a 'Sioni bob ochr' (Johnny every-side).

By the time the prince arrived in Carmarthen, he had visited several places between Caernarfon and there. He was welcomed by thousands and thousands of people in every destination and also along the way. Gwynfor had seen this and had clearly thought it would be a good idea to take advantage of such a popular event in the town where he was the Member of Parliament. But that isn't how the action was seen. Rather, they saw a man who had stuck to his beliefs and made a big fuss about it on 1 July, and then four days later realising his mistake and miscalculation, personally welcomed the prince to Carmarthen.

From my point of view, I didn't have much interest in the Investiture. I didn't see it as an event of any great importance. I am not a great supporter of the Royal family, nor do I believe that the Prince of Wales should come from their midst. I didn't look at the ceremony on the television, and neither did I go to Carmarthen to be with the crowds to welcome the new prince, officially or unofficially. I didn't campaign on the matter, one way or another. To me, it wasn't an electoral campaigning matter at all.. Therefore, I didn't have any principled or political objection to Gwynfor's stance of the ceremony itself. It was his hypocrisy afterwards that I objected to.

Gwynfor believed that the Investiture would benefit Plaid Cymru, and that was his opinion during the weeks following the ceremony. He told Harri Webb that within six weeks, it would be obvious that the Investiture had been of benefit to Plaid Cymru, through awakening nationalism. Rhys Evans's biography of Gwynfor says that he believed things were as good as they were ever for the party in July 1969. The author then says:

With the benefit of hindsight, Gwynfor's confidence as he considers the aftermath of the Investiture appears to be a completely eccentric judgement, but the majority of Plaid Cymru leaders thought the same way.

I was very familiar with Gwynfor's eccentric statements.

In looking back over the period, I can, in one way, clearly see Gwynfor's dilemma. Some argued that Gwynfor would have increased his popularity had he gone to the Investiture and shown support to an event that was obviously so popular throughout Wales. Others argued that in sticking to his principles, by refusing to play the popular game, that would have been advantageous to him. But I don't see it that way. Gwynfor was a politician, and he had a political game to play, not only with the public but within his own Party. Going to the Investiture would have meant making a clear stand against influential members in his own party and also against Cymdeithas yr Iaith. He could scarcely have done that.

To place this action by Gwynfor in its wider context, it was yet another incident to add to the chain started by his attempt to visit Viet Nam, then his attitude towards violent action. Now, a couple of years later came his Investiture debacle. He had been undermining his own position in the eyes of many. Had he been much more careful, strategic, and stronger, Gwynfor could have counteracted quite a few of the jibes and criticisms that people like me, Cledwyn Hughes, George Thomas, John Morris, Denzil Davies, Wil Edwards, Huw Thomas and others would level against him.

THE YEAR OF THE REAL BATTLE!

As the hype of the Investiture died down, and as 1969 came to an end, it became clear that the following year would be the year of the General Election. I had some advantage with regard to knowing when the election was likely to happen as I was on the inside of the party machine and had a close relationship with the parliamentary party at Westminister and the party's headquarters in Transport House, London.

If that was an advantage in one way, it's true to say that they were not good days for the Labour Party. There were three specific cases causing problems for the Party in the constituency. Firstly, the farmers weren't happy with their lot. In a county like Carmarthenshire, that is a central consideration as they worried about payments they were receiving for their produce. The strength of their emotion came to the fore outside Carmarthenshire, when Jim Callaghan, the Home Secretary at the time, went on a visit to west Wales in January 1970. He had a very stormy meeting with the Ceredigion and Haverfordwest farmers, and rotten tomatoes were thrown at him.

Fortunately, Barbara Castle, the Employment Secretary, was on a visit in the west some five weeks later. She succeeded in calming the farmers' fears in a way that Callaghan hadn't. On reporting her visit, a headline in the *Western Mail* sums it up: "Farmers fall for Barbara". There were over 200 farmers in Haverfordwest to welcome her in March 1970. "We want Barbara!" was their call. Her answer, "OK, let me put some lipstick on." It worked. She went to Carmarthen, where she spoke with more farmers. She told officers of the National Farmers' Union that there was a future for small farms, such as the ones in the majority in Carmarthenshire, and that the government wanted to support them as much as they could. Thank goodness for her intervention, to quieten the farmers' very real fears.

The other hot topic was the future of the Defence Ministry's firing range in Pembrey, near Llanelli. I was in favour of moving the Shoeburyness Military Centre to the site in Pembrey. Denzil Davies and Gwynfor Evans were against it. My argument was that such a move would be advantageous to the area for jobs, the economy and it would also ensure the future of the defence site at Pendine. At the time, that site employed up to six hundred people.

This argument continued to drag on into May 1970. That is when I wrote an article in the *Carmarthen Times* on the issue. The headline was one that I was particularly proud of: "We want bread and butter before buckets and spades." That is a clear reference to the main argument of those who were against developing the site as a military one, namely the benefit that would come to tourism in the area. In the article I said:

I for one will not be a party to throwing away valuable jobs and see the depopulation of West Carmarthenshire unless there are overpowering reasons for the Pembrey proposals. As yet I am unaware of such reasons.

Druids of Doom

The Welsh language was the other subject receiving quite a bit of attention at the time. This was the era of the protests against English-only road signs which were defaced or removed. This is the subject that meant Jim Callaghan had a much quieter time away from the Ammanford farmers than he had in Ceredigion. In the Amman Valley, the subjects in question were the law-breaking methods of the language protestors, the imprisonment of Dafydd Iwan and the alleged role of the Special Branch in the nationalistic campaigning. Denzil Davies and I certainly had a harder time in that meeting.

In the months that followed, the language turned into a conspicuous subject in the battle for Carmarthen. I was increasingly attacking Plaid Cymru with my comments. As early as 8 January 1970, a story appeared in the *Carmarthen Times* and the *Carmarthen Journal*. The headline was "Nationalists have not shown they can run a parish council".

> *Addressing his party's constituency management committee, Mr Jones said that since July 1966 too much talk about Wales had been heard from Carmarthen MP Gwynfor Evans and not enough about the constituency. This was reflected in the type of question he asked in the House of Commons. "Let Mr Evans tell us the number of questions he has asked specifically about the constituency," challenged Mr Jones.*

Some weeks later, I was once again highlighting and re-visiting a theme that had been obvious enough since I had been chosen as candidate for the Labour Party, namely Gwynfor's stance on the issue of violence and aggressive action in the name of the Welsh language.

> *It is high time Mr Evans realised that he just cannot say he deplores violence on the one hand, and continue to make irresponsible, emotive statements on the other. He has compared Wales with Lithuania – "oppressed", then that Wales is in a state of "near ruin" and being "whipped" by the English. He has even expressed the viewpoint that only when someone is "shot or blown up" will the government listen...*
>
> *The fact is that too many Plaid Cymru leaders refuse to accept that this government has done anything worthwhile. They depict this government as plotting to "kill" the Welsh language. Let him admit that many measures have been taken to foster the language.*

The suggestion that members of the Labour Party were killing the Welsh language was really hurtful to the number of us within the Party who loved the language and fought for it. We were just as Welsh as everyone else. Reading the Welsh press in those days could create a clear impression that nationalists not only truly believed that the government did nothing at all for the language but that, in reality, it did as much as it could to kill the language.

On more than one occasion, Gwynfor was asked what he believed the Labour Party did for Wales. Without fail, his answer was "Nothing". It was hard to accept such a stance in a period when the Labour government created the office of the Secretary of State while the Language Act was passed in 1967 and the process of allowing local authorities to place bi-lingual road signs began – and that was before the painting of road signs campaign started in earnest.

I often criticised Gwynfor's tendency to abuse the Labour Party. To me, when he did that, he also abused Wales. His custom of painting quite a bleak picture of Wales was unpatriotic. I described Gwynfor and others who were full of negative comments about Wales as "Druids of Doom". They offered Wales no favours by continually denouncing the country.

By the end of 1970, I had turned my attention to the young people of the constituency. In the *Carmarthen Times* on Friday, 27 February, there was quite a bold heading, together with a photo of myself:

Gwynoro Jones – a Welsh-speaking Welshman – says:
Young people are being exploited

In a box at the side of my photo, there was a quotation from the article.

High time so-called lovers of Wales realised that recent antics are driving people further away from the language.

In the story, I argued that young people were being misled by middle-aged men who had failed to do what they now expected the youngsters to do. I warned that such pressure would create a linguistic split in Wales just as religion had created a split in Northern Ireland.

The lesson of Northern Ireland has been that religion has so divided its people that they have been unable to unite to solve far greater problems – bad housing and social conditions.

This article includes a quotation from the Hansard notes on a debate on the Welsh language in Parliament on 16 February:

Mr Gwynfor Evans – *asked the Secretary of State for Wales if he will now seek to raise the Welsh language in Wales to a status of equality with English in Wales.*

Mr George Thomas – *The government have already raised the legal status of the Welsh language in Wales to that of equality with English.*

Mr Evans – *Is the Secretary of State aware that some people may admire the lion-hearted way in which he has stood up, with nothing more formidable than the British government behind him, to the great bully the Welsh Language Society and the way in which he is resisting any advance in Wales to national status? Is he also aware that I am not among his admirers?*

Mr Thomas – *I feel heartbroken by the hon. Gentleman's last remark. I am well aware that the hon. Gentleman does what he can to stir up members of the Welsh Language Society to indulge in the sort of hooligan exercises which we have recently witnessed. I share the opinion of Lord Justice Arthian Davies that they can do nothing but bring shame and disgrace to Wales.*

Mr William Edwards – *Is my right hon. Friend aware that the implicit misrepresentation about the status of the Welsh language in that supplementary question is* *typical of the kind of misrepresentation taking place in Wales by people who should be more responsible and which is leading young people who are misrepresented to take unjustifiable and unwise actions?*

Mr Thomas – *My hon. Friend speaks for a very wide representation of opinion in the Principality. Major constructive steps have been taken in an endeavour to succour the Welsh language, and no good at all will ensue from the sort of militant action of which the hon. Member for Carmarthen (Mr. Gwynfor Evans) is so proud.*

Gwynfor's early stance on militant and aggressive action in the name of the language was still a hot topic. Denzil Davies joined in also attacking Gwynfor, as part of his campaign in the Llanelli constituency. In a newspaper article, he criticised Gwynfor for yet again comparing Wales with another country:

Mr Gwynfor Evans has gone so far as to compare the fate of the Welsh with that of the Lithuanians, who were massacred by Stalin.

Gaining Ground

To Plaid Cymru, the 1970 election was an opportunity to prove that 1966 was not a fluke, and that they had built on the surge of support in Caerphilly and Rhondda West, as well as the successes on various local councils. By March 1970, newspapers in the constituency were talking about the success of the Labour Party. "People Tired of Plaid's Unrealistic Outbursts" said the *Carmarthen Times* at the end of that month, adding:

Increased enthusiasm and the unrealistic outbursts of Plaid Cymru has made Labour the strongest political force in the county.

This was in a period when things were quite difficult for the Labour Party. After that, headlines like "Labour Will Win Back Carmarthen" were much more consistent.

In May 1970, I wrote an article in the *Carmarthen Times* under the incisive headline, "We want bread and butter before buckets and spades".

We have heard a lot of talk about estuarine barrages, about the conservation of beauty, about the potential of Pembrey as a tourist attraction. In fact, we have heard a lot of pie-in-the-sky talk... Let those who object to the Pembrey gun range give viable alternatives. It is their moral duty.

Gwynfor was one of those I was calling upon to offer better suggestions. After visiting Pendine several times, I came to a definite conclusion:

... I am of the opinion that there is not sufficient evidence to oppose the proposed Pembrey range... I am not prepared to throw away 530 jobs at Pendine. Let us not throw away in Carmarthenshire over 1000 permanent jobs between Pendine and the Pembrey proposal, plus 1000 construction jobs for at least five years without making sure there is alternative employment.

That year, in mid-May, the Annual Conference of the Labour Party in Wales was held in Llandudno. On the Friday evening, the national organiser, Ron Hayward, came up to me. I expected him to ask me to begin the singing, as that was traditional in Party events. But no, instead he asked me why I was still in the conference. He explained that Harold Wilson was going to announce the date of the General Election the following Monday. Laura and I stayed in Llandudno that night and then went straight back to Carmarthen early on the Saturday morning. On the Sunday morning, a meeting of the campaign team was called, and I had the opportunity to hint that Harold Wilson would be making an important announcement the following day. Wilson announced that Parliament would be dissolved on 29 May and the Election would be on 18 June.

To all intents and purposes, I had been campaigning non-stop since October 1967. I had been to every fair, carnival, concert, agricultural show in the constituency, and had shaken thousands of hands and kissed hundreds of babies. It became clear to me soon after I was chosen that there was a need to re-connect with the electorate in the constituency, and there was only one way to do that, namely, meeting them face-to-face.

But now, as the real battle began, we needed to change the emphasis and pick up steam. It became clear that it would be a fierce battle. In his speech during a meeting to adopt him as the official candidate for the Election, Gwynfor Evans said:

We can be under no illusion as to the character of the election. It will be a hard fight. Ever since Carmarthen was won for Wales, the Labour party has concentrated on winning it back for Labour. This is why we have seen so many Cabinet Ministers and even the Prime Minister in Carmarthen. But Labour's greatest advantage comes from rigging the election against us on television.

And, of course, it was an opportunity for him to use another of his unfounded sweeping statements:

Every concession made to Wales since the war has been won by the growth of Plaid Cymru.

Complete twaddle.

Both Lloyd Havard Davies, the Conservative candidate, and the broadcaster Huw Thomas, the Liberal candidate, also turned their attention to Gwynfor in their adoption meetings.

First, Lloyd Havard Davies:

If his record since his arrival at Westminster is any guide, then we can truthfully assume that no journey in Welsh history was as purposeless as this.

And then Huw Thomas:

The Welsh Nationalists think with their blood instead of their heads.

The spirit of the campaign to come had been sealed from the first day.

Some days after the adoption meetings at the end of May, there was one interesting announcement. It was in the *Carmarthen Times*:

> *Carmarthen Labour Club was granted an extension of licensing hours until 2am on election night, 18 June, by Carmarthen Magistrates on Monday. The application was made for members wishing to follow the election broadcasts on the club's colour television.*

A young man for the 70s.

THE CAMPAIGN AND THE BIG NIGHT

From the minute the date of the General Election was announced, the Carmarthen constituency received quite a lot of attention in the media. Would Gwynfor be able to keep his hold on the seat? That was the burning question for the press at the time. Many an analysis was made of the nature of the constituency and, naturally, the strengths and weaknesses of the parties, but one sums up the situation quite clearly. Dennis Johnson, from the *Guardian* newspaper, came to the constituency for some days in June. The headline of the article published following his visit was "Carmarthen – Plaid Cymru's magic may have faded".

He briefly described the nature of the constituency, beginning with a précis of the significance of the 1966 by-election, which Gwynfor won.

Thousands of delirious supporters gathered to cheer Mr Evans in what the Nationalists have now come to regard as those rather magical early hours of 15 July 1966... Nothing would be the same again for Wales or Carmarthen said the bright-eyed victor who had even surprised himself. Almost four years later, things don't seem to be quite the same at all.

He went on to say that "Gwynfor... shot his bolt with too much protesting and too little influence on mainstream politics at Westminster".

No one, however, is suggesting that the Nationalists have lost their appeal. They made a profound impact on the intellectuals, with much of the teaching profession totally committed, and much of this influence remains. West Wales still has at the very least, a passionate interest in devolution and detests remote control.

He foresaw that the battle would be a quite close three-way battle, with the Liberals and Plaid Cymru attracting a substantial number of votes, but that it was the Labour Party who would win.

For one thing, Carmarthen has still not shaken free of Lady Megan, whose brinkmanship between Liberal and Labour had the constituency confused right to the end. Because of what happened at the by-election, no one still knows for sure how much of her vote was Labour, how much Liberal (many old Lloyd Georgians still cannot believe she was anything else) and how much Lady Megan.

Another central consideration, as a backdrop to Dennis Johnson's comments, was the nature of the constituency itself. Paper-thin majorities are certainly a historical part of the county's electoral life. In the seven elections between 1928 and 1951, for example, the biggest majority secured by any candidate was 1,279. There was a majority of less than a thousand in four of the elections and one as low as 47.

There were two stories in the *Guardian* that came from conversations Johnson had on the streets of the town. He relates a conversation he had with a councillor:

I'm on the Borough Council, and I was given a lift to some meeting by a colleague who turned up in a Rolls Royce and said, "Here, man, let me shift this straw out of your way first." Folk tale or not, that's Carmarthen.

The second story is more significant. Johnson had several conversations with the Carmarthen farmers, and he relates one with a farmer in an agricultural smock in the town square, a man who was a well-known character in the town on market day. His response to the current Member of Parliament was quite clear and summed up what many believed.

We didn't get ourselves a local MP. We got ourselves a bloody Messiah!

Campaigning and Leaflets

For me, moving into the period of official and formal campaigning was enthralling and an opportunity to unite my day-to-day work in the marketing world with the electoral battle. For one thing, my work with the Labour Party had given me constant opportunities to join meetings with much more experienced political campaigners. This included regular meetings with George Thomas in his work as Secretary of State and also regular contact with Harold Wilson, the Prime Minister, and other ministers.

Some months earlier, I had noticed one Labour candidate in Scotland and his use of striking campaign leaflets. He was standing in South Ayrshire and his name was Jim Sillars. At the time he was a vocal advocate opposing Scottish Home Rule but who would later join and represent the SNP.

I used Sillars's template and prepared two leaflets of my

own, which were in the form of an attachment in a newspaper; one was slightly bigger than the other and concentrated on talking about the Labour Party's successes and policies – the *Labour Election Special*. The other concentrated more on me as a candidate – *Your Labour Candidate*. These were relatively new in electoral battles at the time. I remember emphasising the importance of having an obvious red stripe on the front page of both. The one concentrating on me is bigger than the Party one, with several red stripes on the front. I knew about the effect of using colour, and red especially, on publicity material.

Both publications were bilingual, but not half and half. Using the Welsh language was all important for me, and in the largest leaflet, there was a section dealing specifically with the language. This is the opening paragraph:

In December 1965, Mr James Griffiths, the Secretary of State for Wales at the time, said to the Welsh Grand Committee, that the Labour government would do what was reasonable and practical to give the Welsh language equal parity. Quietly, the Labour government has been silently fulfilling this promise.

Yn Rhagfyr 1965, dywedodd Mr James Griffiths, yr Ysgrifennydd i Gymru ar y pryd, wrth yr Uwch Bwyllgor Cymreig, y byddai'r llywodraeth Lafur yn gwneud yr hyn oedd yn rhesymol ac yn ymarferol i roi dilisrwydd cyfartal i'r Iaith Gymraeg. Yn ddistwr bu'r Llywodraeth Lafur wrthi'n dawel yn cyflawni'r addewid hwn.

I then identified specific examples of what Labour had done for the language, beginning with the 1967 Welsh

Language Act. A big step in the law was removing the legal prohibitions on using Welsh. Following that, it was possible, for example, to use the Welsh language in legal cases in Wales. I identify several other examples, which I have already mentioned in this book.

By the year of the election, I noted on the leaflet that two hundred and thirty of the government's forms were either in Welsh or bilingual. In April of that year, a car tax disc was also available bilingually. I then identified more direct financial support.

Over the last four to five years, the Labour government has been very generous with its grants to the Urdd – over £70,000. Then over £28,000 was given to the Arts Council in order to promote Welsh literature.

Dros y bedair i bum mlynedd ddiwetha mae y Llywodraeth Lafur wedi bod yn hael iawn gyda'i grantiau i'r Urdd – dros £70,000. Yna rhoddwyd dros £28,000 i Gyngor y Celfyddydau er mwyn hyrwyddo llenyddiaeth Gymreig.

I closed this section by saying:

At the end of the day, it isn't the government but the attitude of the people of Wales that will decide the future of the language.

Yn y pen draw nid y llywodraeth ond agwedd y bobl yng Nghymru fydd yn penderfynu dyfodol yr iaith.

I needed to include this section as it angered me that Gwynfor and his followers wanted to give the impression that it was only they who loved the language. The Labour Party had done a substantial amount for the language. And I certainly was enthusiastic about protecting and promoting Welsh. This is a further example of Gwynfor's nonsense in saying that the Labour Party had never ever done anything for Wales.

There was more about me personally in the candidate leaflet. It included a photograph and short biography of me, together with a photograph and biography of my wife Laura, as she played a central part in all the campaigning. She was naturally a political person. In her youth she had been a Plaid supporter, but since my adoption by the constituency she was highly dedicated to winning for the Labour Party in Carmarthenshire. She was an art teacher by profession, until the children came along. I benefited a great deal from her creativity and energy. She was crucial to the whole campaign.

My son, Cennydd, still remembers canvassing with his mother on my behalf, when they came across Gwynfor Evans also out on the streets canvassing. Laura and Gwynfor recognised each other, and Gwynfor came across to my wife and young son to greet them. He shook Cennydd's hand and chatted to Laura. They spoke to each other in Welsh.

One of Laura's strategies was to go out with a group of campaigners to different districts in the constituency during the day, and then we would come together for the public meeting in the evening. Her warm personality and confidence were of great benefit to the campaign team. And that was true for the whole period of my political career from 1967.

Laura, the centre of attention.

The Battle Plan

The campaign team was led by Ivor Morris, a wonderful man who had been with me from the very beginning with twenty local coordinators working for him throughout every district in the constituency. The campaign day would follow the same pattern: campaigning, distributing leaflets and canvassing in some six districts with public meetings in the evening. Every party would publish a programme of the week's visits in the local newspapers through a full-page advertisement.

I enjoyed canvassing, meeting the people, and the public meetings. I did go door-to-door but it wasn't my strength as a campaigner. I never asked people how they intended to vote. My concentration was on coming across as a person they could support, who was energetic and would work for them and the constituency.

The public meetings, my love of discussion and debate, came from my Sunday School days. In the small villages, there would be about a hundred in each meeting, four hundred in the larger villages and towns. Gwynfor's meetings also attracted similar numbers, and Huw Thomas also attracted large crowds in several places, boosted by his ITN profile. Towards the end of the campaign, Huw and I shared the same stage in several public meetings, one speaking after the other, and both had our respective supporters in the audience. One of these occasions was the Tuesday before polling day, in the Town Hall in Kidwelly that was full to bursting. For some reason, there wasn't much discussion between the candidates in those days, and unfortunately, I didn't have a debate with Gwynfor directly.

Over the Black Mountains

Five days before voting, the Conservative Party announced the result of an opinion poll saying that I would win by some two thousand votes. That was also the opinion of the local bookies. I remember that the weather was very sunny during those weeks. It was certainly very fine the night before voting. That was a good thing because we had arranged a cavalcade procession of some fifty cars to travel through the county. We started in Carmarthen, then St Clears and Whitland, along the A40 to Llandeilo and Llandovery, over the Black Mountains towards Cwmllynfell. A thrilling experience was everyone singing hymns on the mountains. From Cwmllynfell on to Brynaman and through the Amman Valley and on to the Gwendraeth Valley. After six hours on the road, there was a public meeting at Ysgol Maes yr Yrfa, Cefneithin. Laura and I were in an open-topped jeep throughout the journey, and my father, who was a carpenter, had made a wooden frame to keep us all safe in the rear, and the Red Dragon flew from it.

Coming into Cefneithin from Gorslas, we could see hundreds of people outside the school. I must admit that it created quite an emotional impression on me, and I began to cry. It was an unbelievable scene, and the welcome by people who had known me since I was a child was thrilling. The willing and constant support of people from my square mile had been a support to me from the beginning.

However, it wasn't a bed of roses in that area. Plaid Cymru had their fervent campaigners there, people like the bard Dai Culpitt and Jac Davies, from the popular duo Jac a Wil. They were friendly enough to me personally but there was one person who had a much more malicious attitude. To begin with, I didn't know who he was. About a year before the election, letters started arriving at my parents' home. They were posted there by people from different places throughout the constituency, as far away as Rhandirmwyn near Llandovery. Those who contacted my parents had received an envelope with "Please Open Me" on them. Inside, there was a piece of paper written in my name, boasting about myself and saying how special I was. I contacted the police, but there wasn't much they could do. Until some months later, we had a visitor from the village to my parents' home. He gave me a letter identifying a subject that needed attention. I at once recognised the handwriting. I didn't say anything to this man, but I contacted the police to ask them to have a quiet word with him. I knew the man well. He was an independent councillor on the Parish Council and a family friend. It's strange what some people are ready to do come election time. I was never sure whether it was born of envy or malice.

I received a very warm welcome in Llangadog, which is Gwynfor's village, of course. I received a significant amount of support there. But Plaid supporters had been busy putting up posters everywhere. I received a telephone call from David Hewitt, a *Western Mail* reporter.

The poster count on the roads and hedges doesn't look good for you, Gwynoro.

My answer was:

According to the hedges, Gwynfor has won, but according to the houses, I have.

The day of the voting was upon us. There is no doubt that the battle was a fierce one, with the local newspapers a platform for the battling. Gwynfor's words at the beginning of the campaign were correct enough: "Let's not kid ourselves – this will be a tough scrap."

Thursday 18 June 1970

As eighteenth of June dawned, there was one obvious change in the usual pattern of voting. The polling stations would be open until ten o'clock at night instead of nine o'clock as it had been until then. Clearly, the aim was to try and get more people out to vote. It must be noted also that this was the first General Election when people had a right to vote at eighteen years of age. I had sent birthday greetings to each one in the constituency as they reached eighteen. The weather was also a great help on polling day. It was a fine sunny day, and it made the work of going around the area with a loudspeaker to urge people to vote much easier.

As the day went along, there was no lack of confidence in the town's Labour Party camp nor in the rest of the constituency. But the same was true of the Plaid Cymru camp. There was a strong eagerness to prove that the victory in 1966 wasn't a fluke, and of course, Plaid's heartening performance in a few elections since then, and their progress in local councils, fed their confidence further.

There isn't much you can do on the day itself. To all purposes, everything has been done. Therefore, after travelling around a little to encourage people to vote, it was time to close the polling stations and start the count. By this time, an enormous crowd had gathered on Guildhall Square, Carmarthen, some thousands, I'm sure. The majority were Plaid Cymru supporters, echoing the scenes on the square four years earlier.

The result was ready by three o'clock in the morning. And this is how the votes of the Carmarthen people were shared:

Lloyd Havard Davies (Conservative) 4,975
Gwynfor Evans (Plaid Cymru) 14,812
Gwynoro Jones (Labour) 18,719
Huw Thomas (Liberal) 10,707

There was no way of hearing the final candidate's result. It was obvious before its announcement that I had won, and the Plaid Cymru supporters weren't happy at all. This was the only seat for the Labour Party to regain in 1970 on a night when they lost over 60 seats throughout Britain. Nationally it was a surprise victory for the Conservatives. Labour were voted out of office.

The atmosphere became quite uncomfortable edging towards bitterness and even violence. This was the *South Wales Echo*'s report on the night:

The hundreds of youngsters who had jammed the square could not believe it. Some of them cried like babies, others shook their fists and jeered the man who had ousted Gwynfor. It had been a feverish election vigil in Carmarthen – perhaps the most tense and highly charged wait polling has produced the length and breadth of the country. Flags and flagons were waved. Fighting broke out in the crowd and fruits started flying. A lot of youngsters were screaming, "If you're not Plaid you must be English".

I was inside the Town Hall most of the evening. It became obvious that the police were concerned about letting me out of the building. The *Echo*'s report carries on:

Just after midnight I got a tip from a policeman that things were likely to boil over when I took cover in an outside broadcast scanner van directly outside the Shire Hall. The scanner van was under pressure, like being under siege. The crowd refused to let Gwynoro Jones be heard as he spoke from the balcony of the old Shire Hall, which houses the assize courts and where some of the most famous murder trials of the last two centuries were heard. But this time, it was the crowd outside who were hollering murder.

Perhaps talking about murder is taking things a little too far, but it does convey clearly the fear felt by many that night. I was prevented from speaking from the hall's balcony because of the crowd's behaviour. That is the norm for the successful candidate of course, but I didn't get the chance. It didn't make much difference to me on the night; tasting the victory was enough.

But the time came to leave the town hall. The police were very unsure whether Laura and I should go out at all. We were told that it wasn't safe for us to go out through the doors and that they couldn't guarantee our safety. I didn't expect the next suggestion, and I must say it made me smile. It was suggested that Laura and I should wear a police uniform so that we could leave un-recognised. I refused that suggestion. In the end, we were taken along narrow corridors towards the back of the building, where murderers such as Ronald Harries had once walked, and there a police car was waiting to take us to the Labour Party Offices in Spilman Street. There was plenty of celebration there. I remember Denzil Davies turning up who had won Llanelli. By five o'clock in the morning, I was ready to go home.

As we got to Foelgastell, with dawn breaking, I saw a crowd outside the Dynevor Arms. My grandfather's brother had bought two barrels of beer, and there were free drinks for everyone. The Dynevor opened on Thursday morning for the voting and stayed open until Saturday night! Hard to countenance but absolutely true. The landlord and landlady of the pub (affectionately called Lady Dynevor) always had close contact with local magistrates and police officers. It is a time that lives in my memory to this day. Unforgettable.

On the balcony 1970.

THE MEMBER OF PARLIAMENT FOR CARMARTHEN

The Friday, of course, was the day of the response. The discussions in the newspapers, on the radio and the television. My comment, when interviewed about the victory, was quoted in the *Carmarthen Times*:

> *This has been a victory for organisation and a readiness to go and meet the people on the doorstep. But of far more importance the people of Carmarthen wanted to show they want to go back into the mainstream of politics. They have grown tired of pessimistic talk.*

Plaid Cymru's response in the same paper was a statement by a speaker on their behalf:

> *We are very sorry. It is sad that Carmarthen people have taken a step back.*

Side by side with that news story was an article by the editor, John Hughes, summing up the situation. He began by saying that the Plaid Cymru supporters were expecting a sweeping victory but their candidate was not as optimistic. He once again quoted what Gwynfor said when he was nominated as a candidate by his party, namely the comment about a hard battle. But he also added Gwynfor's next sentence, which didn't receive much attention at the time.

"Let us be under no illusions," he said in his adoption speech. "It will be a hard fight." And he added: "We have a tremendous amount of leeway to make up."

He then discussed what Gwynfor meant when he said, "leeway to make up". He asked, were some members of Plaid Cymru concerned that Gwynfor only had a small majority in 1966? More than that, was there concern that support for him had lessened since 1966? Clearly, that was what it showed when the 1970 election results were announced. The editorial praises Gwynfor for his untiring work as a Member of Parliament, but then said this:

But the trail he was blazing did not contain sufficient fire to please some of his supporters.

There was quite a bit of analysis in the *Western Mail* on the Saturday following the election. In one article, written by the Welsh Affairs Correspondent, Geraint Talfan Davies, he offered three points to summarise the election results in Wales in 1970.

- *1970 was the lowest Labour poll in Wales since 1945.*
- *Despite a swing of 4.5 per cent from Labour to the Tories in Wales, the Conservatives' percentage share of the poll was lower than in any election since 1950.*
- *Plaid Cymru have overtaken the Liberals in Wales and recorded their highest poll ever, despite losing Mr Gwynfor Evans' seat at Carmarthen.*

Every party's vote was down, apart from Plaid Cymru's. That gives a wider context to Gwynfor's loss in Carmarthen. The Welsh situation also throws some doubt on Gwynfor's comments after he lost, when he said that the electoral broadcasting on television had a negative effect on Plaid Cymru. His quotation "... the election had been rigged against Plaid Cymru by television and deliberately so..." appeared in several newspapers the weekend after the result. Another of Gwynfor's empty sweeping statements.

Another article in the same edition of the *Western Mail* portrays four new Members of Parliament in Wales, Michael Roberts, John Stradling Thomas, Wyn Roberts and myself. It is interesting to note that Wyn's experience of work before that was in the world of television and mine in the world of marketing. It was an early indication of the route politics was to follow. In the section that spoke about me, I am described as "... built like a useful middleweight boxer..." Then the columnist identifies one reason why he thought I had won:

> ... *hands which had knocked on 7,000 doors during a stamina-sapping, three-clean-shirts-a-day doorstep campaign, which he is convinced is a major factor in his victory.*

It said that my victory was "... *quite an achievement...*", echoing Trevor Fishlock's comment that beating Gwynfor would be tantamount to "... *toppling a king...*"

Gwynfor's comment in the same article is:

Plaid Cymru is now well established in the majority of constituencies in Wales as the only challenge to the Labour Party.

The battle between us was sure to carry on. There was an unexpected example of this in *Y Cymro* some weeks later. A verse was published in the paper.

Aeth cawr Llangadog dan y don
Roedd hyn yn anioddefol
Pa hawl oedd gan y werin hon
I wrthod dewis dwyfol.

Roughly translated it says that the giant of Llangadog sank beneath the wave, which was intolerable. What right did the ordinary folk have to reject a "chosen one".

This is a strong echo of the "Bloody Messiah" in the article in the *Guardian*. The work was presented as anonymous, and as a result, for several weeks, there was much speculation about who had composed the verse. Talk was that Elystan Morgan, Cledwyn Hughes and Goronwy Roberts were responsible. In the end, George Thomas said that he had written the verse under the name Siôr O Donypandy. Nobody was willing to believe that George Thomas had done such a thing. One reader challenged the alleged author by offering him £50 if he would appear on one of the BBC's Welsh radio programmes. George accepted the challenge and read the verse on air. From then on it was believed that George was the real author. But a few years ago the truth came to light. George wasn't the author at all – that isn't much of a surprise. The three who were initially believed to have written the verse were the ones that actually did write it – Elystan, Cledwyn and Goronwy! I know because Elystan told me.

Quite a strong cohort did believe that my success was unbearable and that refusing the divine choice even more blasphemous. However, in that first year as a Member of Parliament, my attention was on my new responsibility.

First Speech

Therefore, after a weekend of celebration, up to London I went, then to Westminster. The first duty I had to undertake there was to swear the parliamentary oath. In 1970, Denzil Davies, Caerwyn Roderick, Tom Ellis and myself asked for permission to do so in Welsh. We were refused.

Gwynfor was the first to ask for permission to take the oath of allegiance in Welsh, in 1966 when he was first elected. But he was refused that permission. He took his oath in English. Finally, in the first election of 1974, a few of us newly elected MP's asked again to take our oath in Welsh. This time, unexpectedly and historically, we were allowed to do so. That was the first year that cross party MP's from Wales pledged their oath to the Westminster Parliament in the Welsh language.

The week after the election result four buses full of Labour Party members and supporters came to see me enter Westminster for the first time. They arrived late as my father had insisted on going to find somewhere that sold egg and chips once they had reached London. My father's food tastes were very simple.

After sitting in the chamber, various thoughts turned in my head as I looked around at everyone else around me. "This is where Lloyd George and Nye Bevan sat". *I'm with the youngest here.* I understood later that only Neil Kinnock, Ken Clark and Jeffrey Archer were anywhere near to my age. Then another thought came to the fore, "Well, Gwynfor, you're not laughing at me anymore!"

Wednesday, 22 July 1970, was the date of my first speech in Parliament. I had to wait until very late in the day to make it – 4.37 the following morning to be precise. The subject? Eradicating brucellosis, which is the disease you can catch from milk or cheese that hasn't been pasteurised. It affects cattle and people. This is the beginning of my speech:

I was born and bred in Foelgastell in the heart of the constituency, and it is a long time since Carmarthen people sent to this house one who was born amongst them.

I then spoke about the historical virtues of Carmarthenshire, and said that it was the county of Merlin, the Bishop Farrar, Gruffydd Jones Pantycelyn, where Dylan Thomas lived and where Beca's girls were nurtured.

Carmarthen is a constituency which epitomises the life of Wales – strong in its upholding of the culture, tradition and way of life of the Principality. In it one will find people imbued with the radical tradition, warm in its welcome to strangers, but determined to combat injustice and oppression.

Then came the content for the debate relating to brucellosis, and again based on the situation back in Carmarthenshire, the main milk production county in Wales, where 62 million gallons of milk were produced, which brought in £8 million to the county.

There was a good response to the speech, especially from James Stodart, the Parliamentary Secretary to the Ministry of Agriculture.

He has warmed our hearts. He has made a great impact on this house. He has a great deal to contribute.

A direct result to the contents of the speech was an announcement by the government that west Wales would be included as one of five areas throughout Britain where they would carry out tests to eradicate brucellosis.

I made extensive use of the privilege of speaking in the House and also the presentation of written questions. That was a central element of my work as a Member of Parliament. Between 1970 and 1974, altogether, I asked about seven hundred questions. I made around forty speeches as well as contributions in different committees. In my first year, I asked more questions than Gwynfor did during the whole of the four years he was a Member of Parliament. And the majority of questions asked by him were written ones, as he was rarely in the House of Commons. However, it must be said, I also made so much use of written questions because I saw they had been an effective tool in Gwynfor's tactics. But questions of that sort were not my main tool.

In December 1970, in the *Western Mail* newspaper and

in the *Welsh Political Notebook* column, Anthony Barber, their Westminster correspondent, had written an article summarising my first month as a Member of Parliament. The headline was "Young Mr Jones is soon at his ease". After saying that I was one of the most industrious Members of Parliament, and that was surprising considering I was still in my twenties. In my first interview with him, I listed the facilities there for us:

> *For instance, we new MP's have to ballot for a desk. Personally, I didn't try since some of the members' rooms are so far from the House that there is great inconvenience in being in one of them. At the moment, I do my work in the library or in the Welsh room, and I suppose that this is because it is only four years ago that I left university.*

Devolving Labour

I had been involved with preparing Labour's evidence to the Crowther Commission on the Constitution. When Crowther died, Kilbrandon took over both report and name.

The working party that I chaired in 1969 reported back to the Welsh Executive Committee and the group of Welsh Labour Members of Parliament, presenting our suggestions. Every meeting was contested and they could become fiery. This is when I first began to disagree with George Thomas on aspects of devolution. The objections from a cohort of other Labour Members of Parliament from the Valleys towards our findings was also quite bitter.

On several occasions, in public meetings, Gwynfor said that the Constitutional Commission had only been established because he had won Carmarthen in 1966. That is factually untrue and a Gwynfor fantasy. He also often disregarded the growth effects of Plaid Cymru in Caerphilly and Rhondda West. These were seats that were much more at the heart of the Labour Party than Carmarthen. Election results in those two constituencies in the late Sixties shook the Labour Party more than the result at Carmarthen, even though Plaid candidates didn't win. In Gwynfor's view, only his contribution was important. He also ignored another strong and influential factor – Scotland. Several of Scotland's prominent Labour leaders were strongly supportive of devolution, in contrast to Labour members representing Wales's industrial areas. Without a doubt, there had been considerable pressure coming to establish a commission from Scotland.

Within the Welsh Labour group of MPs in Westminster, there were prominent members of Harold Wilson's government who were in favour of devolution. Cledwyn Hughes, Goronwy Roberts, John Morris and possibly very significantly, Elystan Morgan who was deputy to Jim Callaghan in the Home Office. They were responsible for constitutional matters. I know as a matter of fact that Callaghan asked Elystan what was the best way forward on devolution. He and John Morris had been discussing the possibility of establishing a Constitutional Commission, and that is the answer he offered Callaghan. John Morris recounted in his memoirs *Fifty Years in Politics and the Law*:

Elystan told me... that he believed the answer to our problem was a Royal Commission for Wales and Scotland... I immediately warmed to the suggestion, which was completely new to me.

It took four years for the Commission to publish their report, and that was done eventually on 31 October 1973. The thirteen commissioners offered at least four possibilities for Wales: a legislative assembly – supported by six of the thirteen commissioners, executive assembly, consultative assembly and a nominated body, and two of them published their own minority report. Without a doubt, this was the most detailed and thorough inquiry into governing Britain that had ever been published. It is quite possible that this is still true.

In April 1969, when Harold Wilson announced that he wanted to establish such a Commission, Plaid Cymru's response was to call it a "charade" and a "denial of the natural aspirations of the people of Wales". After publishing its report, Plaid Cymru called it an *"important step forward"* and that the first months following publication would be "the most fateful in two thousand years of Welsh history". This had not surprised me at all. I was more than familiar with Gwynfor speaking first and then thinking later, predicting dark days and then taking the praise for any good news.

I had been involved in Labour's acrimonious devolution debate since 1967 and aware that Jim Griffiths, for example, had called for an Elected Council for Wales long before he became Secretary of State. It had then been official policy of the Labour Party since 1966. John

Morris, Cledwyn Hughes, Goronwy Roberts and Elystan Morgan, the four were Ministers in the government at the time and played a very prominent part in establishing the Commission in the first place.

The Prime Minister must publish a Green Paper immediately and this must contain a commitment to establish a Welsh government with legislative powers before the end of the present Parliament.

This call came from within the Labour Party in the mid-sixties.

Of course, we must accept that, within the Labour Party, opinion was not unanimous. The records showed that my working group's recommendations in late 1969 to establish a legislative body were originally much stronger than the evidence eventually presented to the Kilbrandon Commission by the Labour Party in Wales. The group wanted a proper legislative assembly. But after reading our recommendations, what was agreed within the Labour Party in Wales was an elected council with administrative powers only.

In a speech and an article in November 1973, with Kilbrandon receiving quite a bit of attention, I discussed one specific point in the Commission's Report, relating to people's attitude towards increasing regional responsibilities throughout Britain. The figures showed that there was more of a demand for regional independence in nine areas in England than there was here in Wales. For example, 60% wanted devolution for Yorkshire and 57% in Wales. In December, I wrote an article saying that once a long-winded debate started, regarding the differences between a legislative or an executive role for an Assembly in Wales, then those who were against Devolution would use the differences as an excuse to do nothing at all. I could scarcely have realised the implications of such a comment, namely the debacle of the 1979 Referendum.

On a more personal level, it was very difficult to accept accusations that spoke about a lack of commitment on my part towards Wales and the Welsh language. I was in a good position to actively debate the cause for devolution for Wales within a system that could do something about it. And I was doing that with zest and conviction. I was receiving accusations of being a nationalist from within my own party and was being accused of being anti-Welsh by Plaid Cymru. Something wasn't right somewhere. There were some within the Labour Party who were one-eyed and some within Plaid Cymru who were blind. I was a nationalist, but within the Labour Party.

This raises another point. Gwynfor never attacked, nor judged, the Conservative Party. The Labour Party was his only target. That became obvious when I was a candidate and then a Member of Parliament. If he had declared that the Labour Party hadn't done anything for Wales, then he didn't make such statement regarding the Conservative Party. On one occasion, I decided to do some research into the Tory's record in Wales, in order to see what exactly Gwynfor wasn't condemning. This is what I discovered at the time:

During the thirteen years of Tory rule between 1951 to 1964, 70 per cent of railway stations and halts in Wales

were closed, a total of 800 miles of rail line. In 1951
there were 730 stations and halts in Wales. In 1964
only 215 remained open.

I compared this with only five miles of track being closed
by the Labour Party between 1964 and 1970. But yet
again, the leader of Plaid Cymru was accusing Labour of
destroying the Welsh railway service. The same was true
about spending on Wales's road network. When Labour
came to power, there were plans in place to improve roads
in Wales, based on an expenditure of £17 million. By the
time I became a Member of Parliament in 1970, expenditure on roads in Wales was up to £50 million. But, of
course, it was Gwynfor who was "Mr Dual-carriageway".

Gwynfor's abusive attitude towards the Labour Party was
clear in a conversation he had with Elystan Morgan back
in 1965, the period when Elystan was considering leaving
Plaid Cymru in order to join the Labour Party. When discussing this with Elystan, Gwynfor's reaction was:

You know what you're doing don't you? You're joining
Bessie Braddock's party!

Bessie Braddock was a Labour Member of Parliament for
Liverpool, a typical working-class character from that city.
She was called "Battling Bessie" because of her untiring
commitment, but she never had a ministerial responsibility in all the time she was a Member of Parliament. She
was truly one of the working classes. In an opinion poll,
she was chosen as the second most popular woman in
Britain after the Queen.

Elystan knew only too well who Bessie Braddock was, and not only because of her public popularity. Bessie and her husband were active members of Liverpool Borough Council in the period when there were discussions about drowning Cwm Celyn which sparked the Tryweryn protesting. Gwynfor had been to one of the Council meetings at that time, and Bessie and her husband were also there. It was a fiery meeting and talk is that Gwynfor had to leave.

It is natural enough that this connection is in Gwynfor's mind as he makes the observation. But that doesn't change the fact that he chose her as an example to identify when speaking with Elystan, nor lessening any blow in the spirit the words were spoken. He wanted to shame Elystan for joining a party of "someone like Bessie". His observation showed failure to identify with Bessie and the values which she represented. He was hardly ever for the ordinary working person, his was of a different upbringing and philosophy.

It was an obvious and deliberate tactic by Plaid Cymru to target rural seats. On a political level, I can understand that well. Railways and coal mines were closing, unemployment was increasing, Wales was being ignored by London. As a result, it was natural that they wanted to target the constituencies of Carmarthen, Meirionnydd and Caernarfon and attract votes from the Conservatives and Liberals in order to bring the Labour Party down. It was a fair enough political tactic to target a party in this way and for these reasons. But that isn't the whole picture. It is still strange that Gwynfor never once condemned the Conservative Party. He was especially quiet during the period of Ted Heath's Tory government, as he was of the Tories' record between 1951 and 1964. Yes, this was a period of increasing strikes, a three-day working week, rubbish not being collected and all a result of flagrant industrial dissatisfaction. Despite such a period, Gwynfor didn't say that *"Wales is in a state of ruin"* as he did when Labour was in power before Heath. There were no complaints that two of the ministers in the Welsh Office had constituencies in England. There is no doubt that there would have been a considerable amount of protesting had the Labour Party done that.

One conclusion I came to in observing Gwynfor's politics was that there wasn't much doubt, that, at best, Gwynfor was an old-fashioned right-wing Victorian Liberal. At his worst, Gwynfor was a secret Conservative. Such an observation became a clear accusation of Gwynfor's politics long before he became a Member of Parliament, and long before I became involved with him. There is an example of this in D. Ben Rees's biography of Jim Griffiths, the Member of Parliament, *Arwr Glew y Werin*:

> It was a perilous civil war after Gwynfor Evans decided to join the Council's Independent group. The Independent group was a coalition of Liberals and Conservatives and a few who didn't know which ideology to support. To the Labour Councillors of the Llanelli constituency, Gwynfor's behaviour savoured of Conservativism at its worst. There was a huge chasm between the mode of thinking, attitude, background and experience of the Councillor from Llangadog and that of the Labour Councillors of the coalfields.

Lord Elystan Morgan commented on the same point. Here are three quotations from his biography:

> *Gwynfor's attitude was not dissimilar to that of Saunders Lewis with regard to his enmity towards the Labour Party... In my opinion, it is true that Gwynfor despised the Labour Party, and that is one of his inherent weaknesses... he was a right wing Liberal, with a great deal of respect and admiration towards the Conservative Party.*

During Gwynfor's last year as a Member of Parliament, there were one hundred and six votes in the Parliament. Gwynfor only exercised his right to vote in twenty of those, and on sixteen occasions, he voted with the Conservatives. This says quite a lot about his record and the direction of his political beliefs

Taliesin and Llangyndeyrn

As a Member of Parliament, very local matters were my main concern: roads, railways, farming, low flying etc. I was very keen to underline the point that Gwynfor and I were "poles apart", as the newspaper article said. I had no thoughts about considering myself as the Member for Wales.

One of the first local subjects for me to become involved in came from the heart of my roots in the Gwendraeth Valley. I came to the middle of the battle that had been going some seven years. It was a battle about a "record book" in the campaign to fight against drowning the village of Llangyndeyrn. One of the most prominent

leaders of that successful campaign was the Reverend
W.M. Rees. When he moved from the village to Aberdare,
after winning the battle, he gave his record book to the
National Library of Wales. But Carmarthen District
Council wanted the book back for the County Archives. I
was asked to intervene, and I arranged to meet with the
Librarian of the National Library. There was no way in the
world they were going to give that book to anyone. On
top of that, they couldn't give it to anyone without permission from W. M. Rees, who donated the record book
to them in the first place. A compromise was offered. The
library was willing to photocopy the records carefully and
also bind them professionally. I passed on the message to
the District Council. I didn't hear a word after that;
therefore, I expected that they must have been quite
satisfied.

In the October following the election, a particularly
bitter article was published in the magazine *Taliesin*.
There was some criticism of me in it, but the main clout
was against the people of Carmarthenshire for choosing
me and refusing Gwynfor.

It makes us thankful that DJ, JE, JR, T.I. Ellis and Trefor
Morgan to name only five, did not live to see the name
of this constituency degraded not merely to dust but to
depths of a wasteland… We now know the real quality
and value of the constituency which we were foolish
enough to believe had awakened.

A renowned village like Llanddowror; it is completely
dead culturally; St Clears – which pretends to be a
village in Hampshire; Carmarthen itself – a town which

hates to hear a word of Welsh except on market day, and a place – like every old garrison town – which dotes on all sorts of bumph and royal ballyhoo. Llandeilo is exactly the same.

You could almost hear the voice of Caradog Evans in such descriptions. Naturally enough, I made extensive use of the local press to respond to such an article. "Carmarthenshire", I said, "was one of the most Welsh counties in Wales". I added, "When I was canvassing, I spoke Welsh 70% of the time on the streets and in meetings". In an article in the *Carmarthen Times* on 9 October 1970, I was quoted:

I am astounded at the attitude shown. The bitterness expressed because the Nationalist candidate lost the election stems from the belief such people hold of their own importance. They think that they alone are mindful of the problems of Wales. It is indeed time that they were told that there is no monopoly of working for Wales.

The quotation then turns to capital letters, as though I had raised my voice when saying the words:

THERE ARE THOUSANDS OF PEOPLE WHO VOTE FOR THE LABOUR, LIBERAL AND CONSERVATIVE PARTIES WHO ALSO LOVE WALES, ITS CULTURE AND TRADITIONS.

It was an opportunity for me to highlight the lack of facts in comments made in the name of the Nationalists. In writing such comments, a very slack relationship was expressed between the author and real facts. It was empty rhetoric, on a par with Gwynfor's propensity for making sweeping statements.

I went further with my response:

> *Our people might not read the propaganda the Nationalists desire them to read, nor perhaps idolise the people they do. But that is not to say that the people of our constituency are not lovers of Wales and the language.*

A very personal comment about me also appeared in *Taliesin*. In continuing to talk about the people of Carmarthenshire, they say:

> *... they wanted no Welshman, but one who was as materialistic, as rootless and as mistaken as they themselves.*

Clearly, whoever wrote this, believed that only one type of Welshman existed, and I wasn't one of them. I needed to respond to that:

> *I need no lecture from anyone on how to be a Welshman. And certainly not on how to work for the constituency of my birth.*

In another newspaper I identified a few different points:

> *As a Member of Parliament for this constituency, and one born and bred there, I feel it is my duty to tell these*

people not to be so arrogant in their assertions. The quality of the people in our constituency has not deteriorated just because the Nationalists have lost the election. Our constituency has a fine history, and it epitomises the culture, tradition and history of our nation. The bitterness of the article turns sour when it questions the Welshness of the constituency.

I cannot for the life of me understand the arrogant, pretentious attitude amongst Plaid Cymru senior followers that gave the strong impression that they alone were the real Welsh people, and that if you weren't with them or one of them, you were anti-Welsh. Unbelievable. Without a doubt, this is a continuing real stumbling block for Plaid Cymru in this era, and Gwynfor was an earlier incarnation of it.

SIGNS AND MINISTERS

The early years of the Seventies were quite flammable with protests and campaigns relating to the language. Croeso Chwe Deg Nain, *Welcome '69*, with a play on Nain as the north-Walian word for grandmother, had turned into I'r Gâd!, *To Arms!* But, in 1971, my first contribution to the language debate was one that was outside Wales. I argued that the Treaty of Rome, which was the basis for the European Common Market, should be translated into Welsh. My point was that the Common Market would have a significant effect on Wales and on its farmers in particular. Therefore, it was important to ensure that people understood what was happening and how the Common Market worked. Because a substantial number of the Welsh population spoke Welsh, I believed that it was important for them to be able to read the Agreement in Welsh.

There was much letter writing about this in the newspapers. Many supported me. But there was one clear theme to these supportive letters. Their authors were strongly against the protests of the time in the name of Cymdeithas yr Iaith etc., but were willing to accept a request for documents and legislation in Welsh. This is one letter from the *Evening Post* which shows this:

The tragedy these days is that any reference to parity of language is unfairly tainted with a degree of suspicion and disrepute. This is because sign daubing and the almost ritualistic burning this week of English-only

119

licenses, takes away much of the credibility from those who possess an honourable cause.

This is by a person who welcomed seeing the Treaty of Rome in Welsh. But of course, the fiercest debate was between me and the supporters of Cymdeithas yr Iaith, Gwynfor in their midst.

Early in 1971, in March, I spoke at two specific meetings to call on the Secretary of State for Wales to establish a permanent Commission for the Welsh language. I did this at meetings in Llangadog and Brynaman. My point was that creating such a body would provide an opportunity to act practically on the principle of equality for the Welsh language as ensured by the Welsh Language Act of 1969. I called on Welsh people from every party to alleviate the passion that too often overflowed and to give up playing politics with the language. I was quoted in the newspapers:

I am becoming increasingly convinced that one essential need is for the issue to be brought from the realms of party politics. The language, its survival and encouragement are greater than any political gain for any person or party. Everyone should now work for the loosening of the tension that surrounds the concern over the future of our national language, and when I say this, it means that those who want to progress at a quicker rate than hitherto must display a degree of patience and understanding, whilst those in authority, be they in local or central government, must acquire a greater sense of understanding and urgency than hitherto.

My suggestion was that the proposed commission should advise every level of government on how to ensure practical equality for the Welsh language.

I had a particular opportunity to debate such a case following some court cases against members of Cymdeithas yr Iaith. After a number of members of the society, including people like Gwynfor's daughter Meinir and Dafydd Iwan, were jailed because of their law-breaking activities, my attention was drawn towards one central aspect of their life in prison. They were not allowed to speak Welsh with those who had come to visit them. The argument was that the prison officers couldn't understand what was being said and that could be a security risk. This came to the fore in the case of four women who were in Pucklechurch prison and one theological student from Bangor who was in Cardiff prison. I made a request to speak to the Governor of Cardiff Prison because I came to understand that there was a Welsh-speaking prison officer working there. My request was refused. But I disagreed fiercely with a stance that didn't allow someone to speak their mother tongue. The change in the law would be a long time in coming. It was 1993 that the Welsh language act introduced some rights to use Welsh in prisons in Wales and 2011 The Welsh Language (Wales) Measure finally introduced comprehensive rights to use the Welsh language in prisons. The Welsh language has no rights in prisons outside Wales.

I also declared my support for bilingual road signs. I called on the committee established by the Welsh Office to research into the issue of bilingual signs not to take too long to announce their results. I was worried about the cost of providing bilingual road signs, and I suggested that such a process should be undertaken gradually over a period to lessen the financial burden. The ending of one newspaper article that carried this story was:

> But above all there is need to stop this talk of "them" and "us" in relation to the language.

Of course, it was impossible to avoid *them* and *us* in Wales and another example of it became clear when a public spat occured between a number of Welsh ministers of religion and me, which became more a case of *them* and *me*. A large number of ministers, from the Independent Union, decided to make a public stand over some of the law-breaking methods used in the name of promoting the language, specifically on the issue of bilingual road signs and the call for a Welsh-language television channel. The ministers, for example, urged their congregations not to pay their television licence, in order to pressurise the government into establishing a Welsh-language channel.

A letter was written to the press, signed by forty ministers, that declared the need to challenge the law in order to ensure a better status for the Welsh language. This debate lasted for several years. One letter in my collection of newspaper cuttings from June 1974, a good three years since the argument raised its head in the first place. The heading on that letter clearly shows the author's opinion, and it is quite provoking. "Next claim will be that Jesus Christ died for Plaid Cymru!" If you're going to say it.

I was strongly against the ministers' stance. I believed that they went completely against the Bible's teaching on the relationship between faith and politics, as well as a minister's role. If the ministers' arguments were being aired from the pulpit, then it was going completely against the nonconformist tradition that was rooted in the belief that the pulpit should not be used for politics. I was very clear in my objection to these ministers.

> *Indeed, one is tempted to say that the sooner some of them leave our chapels the healthier the situation will be. It is high time they realised that there are people of all political persuasions inside their chapels, and their calling should transcend all party-political talk. They have done far more harm to the religious cause this week than anything else for many a year.*
>
> *Equally disturbing is the call of these ministers to break the law on television licences and yet how many of them are quite prepared to take fat cheques for appearing on television themselves.*

The ministers were furious. They released a press statement, calling on Harold Wilson to reprimand one of his Members of Parliament for trying to threaten and divide leaders and members of the Christian Church. The statement was signed by twenty-four ministers.

In the article in the *Carmarthen Times*, which includes the ministers' comments and a list of their names, on 13 October 1972, there are also further quotations from my response:

... there are names connected with the statement who are active supporters of, and others active workers for, Plaid Cymru. Indeed, I have seen some of them campaigning in elections held in Wales during the last few years. So, I am far from impressed by their assured impartiality.

Hard on the heels of the ministers, came Plaid Cymru's response. According to Plaid's organiser in Dyfed, Peter Hughes Griffiths, I hadn't behaved with the dignity and responsibility expected of a Member of Parliament. According to Gwynfor, in answering my comments, Christianity encompassed every aspect of life, and in this respect, a minister had the right to enter the world of politics. He ends his observations by referring to me:

...the sooner one capable of such affrontery leaves politics, the healthier the situation will be.

Naturally, the debate caught the press imagination, and there was much letter-writing on the matter. Gwynfor contributed to the debate in the press, in a letter to the *Carmarthen Times* in 1973.

The Welsh language is the vehicle of the great Welsh Christian tradition. To uphold this Christian tradition is the duty of all Christians in Wales, to ensure that the values embodied in it are transmitted to future generations is an especial responsibility of the Church.

The symbolic action of the ministers was a courageous act of leadership in this at a time of acute crisis in Wales. The relevance of the language to Welsh Christianity is il-

luminated by the fact that 75% of Welsh-speaking people are members of a Christian Church; of monoglot English-speaking persons, the proportion is about 15%.

Of course, there is no mention of the source of his statistics. And 15% sounds very low to me, remembering how many chapels and churches would have been open in those days.

In October 1972, there is one letter by someone from Lampeter, summarising those who objected to Gwynfor and the ministers' stance.

If ministers of religion want to preach politics let them share platforms with political speakers of any party, not attempt to use the cloth or a place of worship as a means of undue persuasion. If they consider it their duty and right to do so then chapel members have an equal right and duty to express resentment. True Christianity has no barriers, least of all language, and the sooner some of these ministers realise it the better for all concerned. Mr Gwynoro Jones is right. We cannot praise the Lord and attack the television service in the same breath and with the same conviction.

The *South Wales Guardian* was also at the centre of the debate. In October 1972, under the headline "The Union of Welsh 'Inconsistents'", the letter refers to the campaign not to pay for a television licence in particular; it was written by "Cymro" from Garnant. It questions the campaign to withhold payment of the television licence now that an Independent Television Authority was being established in Wales.

This suggests that such Christians would view the Welsh programmes transmitted at present without paying. Is this the Christianity that the minister's referred to preach every Sunday?

I suggest that the Christian way to protest is for all who feel the need for the Authority referred to disconnect their television sets when the current licence expires and put them away until the said Authority is set up for Wales.

This would ensure that all (especially the so-called Christians) would not be viewing programmes free of charge, which would be un-Christian.

Gwynfor's letter, quoted from above, also refers to another incident from the same story that involves me. In 1973, I was invited to appear on the television programme *Heddiw* on BBC Wales to discuss the ministers' argument. I refused. Gwynfor and his supporters latched on to that fact immediately as a sign of cowardice on my part. Gwynfor was to have been on the programme to debate against me. You can imagine the accusations – everybody turning around the fact that I was afraid to face Gwynfor directly. If people had bothered to ask me directly about my reasons for not taking part in the discussion, they would have heard a different story that happened to be true.

I took part in a television programme, half an hour long, on the argument with the ministers. That was on one of the programmes for *Yr Wythnos* on HTV. There were also two ministers on that programme. After it was televised, the BBC decided that they should also give some attention to the debate, but as a three-to-four-minute item on

Heddiw. I didn't see any point in contributing a few minutes a week after debating the matter in detail for half an hour. The fact that the BBC had invited Gwynfor to the item was also an additional factor. I told the BBC I would consider contributing to their programme if they asked one of the ministers to contribute and not Gwynfor. I asked what the justification for that could be. I couldn't understand their choice at all. Their answer was that he was Treasurer of the Independents' Union in Wales! My reply was, "I wonder would they rather invite a member of the Welsh rugby team to contribute to a sporting item or ask the Treasurer of the Welsh Rugby Union. Or perhaps more relevant, ask the Treasurer of the Labour Party in Wales to contribute instead of me!"

In his letter, Gwynfor expresses his disappointment that I hadn't contributed. My stance was defended in the *Carmarthen Times* by Dr Roger Thomas, a member of the Labour party from Capel Hendre and who was to play a much more prominent role in the story in years to come. In his letter, he says:

Of the three dozen ministers involved in activity which had aroused the criticism of Mr Jones, not one had been favoured by being invited to defend their actions. This was at least how the bright boys of the BBC read the situation...

Mr Jones's refusal to appear was fully justified, and I admire this as an example of the political acumen he is fast acquiring.

Mr Evans's appearing on this programme was meant to further his own political cause. That he has people of influence, highly sympathetic to his cause, in the current affairs presentation of Welsh Language television has never been more clearly highlighted.

Escape and Disillusion

When it was a matter of the role of the Welsh language and devolution for Wales, in my political career, T.H. Parry-Williams got it right: "It really was *'ni allaf ddianc rhag hon'*, I cannot escape from this!" Of course, it was true of my involvement with Gwynfor and Plaid Cymru, and also in my involvement with a particular faction within my own party. Early in my career as a Member of Parliament, I came to see that I couldn't identify with a number of my fellow Welsh Members of Parliament in their attitude towards devolution and the Welsh language. There were strong and definite echoes of the responses from within my own party when I suggested that there was a need for an independent Welsh Labour Party, shortly after I was chosen as a candidate for the first time.

Whilst the protesting of Cymdeithas yr Iaith carried on, and Plaid Cymru's nationalistic campaigning, many Labour Members of Parliament were complaining that the Welsh language was receiving too much attention. To people like Neil Kinnock, Alan Williams, and Leo Abse, Roy Hughes and others, there was too much emphasis placed on the ability to speak Welsh, and more specifically, that speaking the language offered some advantage to candidates for major public appointments in Wales. After hearing this complaining for some time, I decided to present a number of parliamentary questions asking some of the government departments how many Welsh-speaking Welsh people they employed.

Slowly, the answers came back and this was the situation. The Welsh Office employed 130 Welsh speakers, which was 13.5% of their staff. The Department of Employment employed 316 Welsh-speaking people, 18.5% of their staff. The figures didn't show any favouritism towards Welsh speakers. The only exception was the Department of Agriculture. They employed 600 Welsh speakers, 45% of their staff. It was easy to understand that, many of the staff of that ministry worked in rural areas where there was a high percentage of Welsh speakers. Not that these figures silenced Kinnock and his like. The language wasn't important to them, whatever the figures were.

It wasn't only in matters such as language and nationalism, where my party and I went in different directions. Within some six months of reaching Westminster, I saw that the Labour Party was a very broad church and that there was nothing at all in common between myself and many of my fellow Members of Parliament. There was nothing to unite me with militant union leaders and the far left-wing Labour Members of Parliament. My world wasn't theirs. When people came to realise this, they took it for granted that I was to the right-wing of the Labour Party. But no. I was never on any right-wing. I was coming to understand that I was liberal at heart, a social democrat by instinct. For many years now though I have perceived myself to be a Welsh radical.

There are two clear areas where I saw things differently to the majority of my party at the beginning of the Seventies: coal and Europe.

In 1972, we had the first official strike in the coalfields

since 1926. The bone of contention was a pay rise, and after the discussions failed, a strike was called, lasting seven weeks. Then, at the end of 1973, there was another dispute between the miners and the government about pay. To save coal, the Prime Minister, Edward Heath, introduced a three-day working week. There was a reduction in the use of electricity in the home, every television station had to finish broadcasting at 10.30 every night, and the pubs had to close earlier than usual. These measures came into force on 13 December 1973. The National Union of Mineworkers voted for another strike in January 1974. That is when I strongly opposed the NUM's stance. I remember hearing Mick McGahey, the fervent Unionist, saying in a speech that if the army were called to break the strike, then they should ignore the call and stay in their barracks or join the picket line. Such a comment was completely against the grain for me. One hundred and eleven Labour Members of Parliament signed a statement condemning his comments, me amongst them.

It was a matter of consistency. I had criticised Gwynfor for not condemning a violent protest in the name of nationalism. I had criticised some Welsh ministers for urging law-breaking from the pulpit. There was no way in the world I could then support law-breaking in the miners' cause. That is what I also did during the miners' industrial dispute in 1971, when there was much debate as to whether there should be a ballot before striking. Constitutionally, there had to be a ballot. But many within the Labour Party were willing to support a strike without a ballot. I didn't support striking without a ballot. That was my constant stance, whatever the subject. Democracy mattered to me as did one member one vote whether within a trade union or the Labour Party.

I firmly believed that what was needed was a change to the law and not to break it. I didn't receive unanimous support for this stance from my party in my constituency. Many were disappointed that I hadn't supported the miners and had not understood that it was the law-breaking I was opposed to, not the miners' stance. But it caused a split amongst my supporters. I then made things worse by criticising Tony Benn publicly, more than once.

On the matter of Europe, things were easier, as the majority of my constituency were against joining the Common Market, as were most Welsh people and myself also. The issue that caused the split between me and my party was the calling for a referendum on the matter. This is what I said in a speech to the Farmers' Union of Wales in 1971:

The question of joining the Common Market should be put to the people in either a referendum or a general election.

In the same speech, I linked membership of the Common Market with Wales's situation specifically.

Those who are calling for the entry to the Common Market must also accept far greater devolution to Wales and Scotland. An elected Assembly to be responsible for many matters relating to Wales will have to be established, so as to counteract the remoteness not from Westminster, but from Brussels.

Who is Governing?

As 1973 came to an end, the Conservative government called for a snap budget. In an article in the *Carmarthen Times* on 21 December, I said that the only purpose in doing such a thing was to make things easier to call a general election. I argued that it was the government's responsibility to try and solve the industrial dispute the country was in, and not to try and tear and divide factions of society against each other.

> *The country faces its gravest economic crisis since 1931... ordinary people, farmers, miners and the rest, have seen costs rise at an unprecedented rate and are looking for an amelioration and bridge the divisions that exist. There are sinister elements on the extreme left and right of politics which are ready to undermine our parliamentary system if given the opportunity.*

I wrote to the Prime Minister, Ted Heath, challenging him not to play politics with the miners' dispute.

> *I urge you to cease looking at the dispute in terms of political advantage. It will be to your eternal discredit if you were to engineer a possible election victory at the expense of doing untold damage to mining and the coal industry, which will cause havoc with the economy.*

In the middle of all this, Gwynfor published a book, *Wales Can Win*. Many of his comments in the book infuriated me.

German invaders could not have caused more than a fraction of the havoc to Welsh national life than the British system had been wreaking for generations.

He made similar comments when Russia attacked Czechoslovakia. He alleged then that the oppression that Wales suffered at the hands of the English was much worse. In referring specifically to the Second World War, he said:

At a time when the vast majority of their fellow countrymen had been brainwashed by Britishness... to ask them to kill their fellow human beings for England in these circumstances was, they felt, to become murderers.

In the local newspapers, I attacked such comments:

Gwynfor cannot accept that in both World Wars, a great deal was at stake for the people of Wales, but according to him, these wars were waged "not to defend anything of great value to Wales".

Nothing of any value? What about family life? Freedom of speech? Religious freedom? And then, I turned to a comment about soldiers from Wales being turned into murderers.

Murderers he called the Welsh soldiers. Well, those tens of thousands of Welsh people fought to ensure our security today... to guarantee a Welsh way of life could exist and guaranteed its survival so that politicians like Gwynfor Evans and Gwynoro Jones can discuss important issues facing Wales today without fear of persecution or imprisonment.

I had predicted correctly. Seven weeks later, the miners' strike started, and two days after that Ted Heath called a General Election for the 28th of February 1974, whilst the three-day week was still in force. There was another battle facing me therefore, but scarcely could I have foreseen what sort of battle it would be.

Homelife: Laura, I and the children.

THE THREE-VOTE VICTORY

Ted Heath's tactics were obvious. He said that the miners were responsible for Britain's economic situation. They were on strike, people had to put their electricity off at night and live by candlelight, and the working week was only three days instead of five. But creating a serious economic situation was not the only accusation against the miners. Much worse than that was alleged. According to the Conservatives, the miners had a deliberate plan to overthrow the government as part of their political ideology. One of those who made the most noise about the miners' plan was Wyn Roberts, Member of Parliament for Conwy. He was regularly on the radio and television talking about the National Union of Miners' various plans, under their militant officials, to destroy the government.

Hundreds of workers in my constituency worked in the coal mines at Cynheidre, Cwmgwili and Abernant. I decided that I should visit them to seek the workers' opinions. Whilst underground at Cwmgwili, I thought about Wyn Roberts's comments.

If he had been with me, he would be much more careful about what he says. These people to whom he was referring are ordinary people who have lived ordinary lives in the ordinary valleys of Carmarthenshire and elsewhere, who have nothing of the sort in mind and want only to make a decent living and give of their best for their country as they have done for decades past.

It wasn't the miners' stance that was mainly responsible for Britain's economic situation at the time. The way to answer Heath's accusations was through showing how the economy had worsened since he took the helm. Britain's debt had increased substantially since 1970, prices were rising very quickly, and the Pound had gone down in value.

Since the miners' strike in 1972, Plaid Cymru had failed to identify with the workers' cause. This was how Rhys Evans in his book on Gwynfor summarises the situation up to the end of 1973. He wrote about this in the context of the by-election in Merthyr in 1972, where there was strong disagreement about choosing Emrys Roberts as a candidate. Many in Plaid, including Gwynfor, were not happy with the choice. But Emrys Roberts fought the election and did very well there.

His achievement, more than anyone, was coming so close to flooring Labour in April 1972. Labour's differences in Europe were also in his favour, but Gwynfor ignored all this. He considered the Merthyr result as a turning point, but Gwynfor, like many in his own party, misread the climate. Merthyr would be the peak of Plaid Cymru's popular growth, not a deposit on further success to come.

He then talks about the effect of this on Plaid Cymru.

After 1972, Plaid Cymru's support in the valleys ebbed – not least as a result of the presence of young energetic leaders in the Welsh Labour party such as Elystan Morgan and Gwynoro Jones. But Gwynfor himself was also responsible for hastening these tendencies and for failing to maintain the support seen for Plaid Cymru in the valleys between 1967 and 1972.

The focus of Gwynfor and his party was obvious – Carmarthen, Meirionnydd and Caernarfon. Those were the only areas that were important to him. That is why he only targeted the Labour Party because they were the only threat in those areas. That is also why he didn't bother with other areas that weren't as Welsh-speaking. A sign of this was the channelling of Plaid's energies towards Cymdeithas yr Iaith and their various activities. In the days of the dispute and strike by the miners and arrant discussions on the Common Market, Gwynfor didn't have very much to say. His focus was on road signs and television licensing. Rhys Evans said that this was of more help to Cymdeithas yr Iaith than it was to Plaid Cymru. Gwynfor missed the opportunity to take advantage of his own party's popularity in the south Wales Valleys because he had a completely personal agenda to follow.

Back to Knocking Doors

I knew that the 1974 election campaign would be completely different to the 1970 one and for several reasons. To start with, there was only a short period of time between the announcement and the election itself. I was in a very strong position in the years leading up to 1970, working within the Labour Party and active in the constituency, in a period when most of the matters relating to the constituency favoured me. I also had Gwynfor's unwise and superficial comments and allegations in my favour, as well as an energetic and enthusiastic team.

In 1974, the political climate did not favour me at all. A substantial faction of the Labour Members of Parliament considered me an opponent because of my stance on devolution. Also, with Britain's miners on strike, I was known as a moderate MP within the Labour Party, one of the seventy who had sided with Roy Jenkins, to whom I was to become Parliamentary secretary. That attachment was to become more clear, public and formal in a few years when forming a new political party, the Social Democratic Party. That story has been well covered in another book *The Forgotten Decade* that was co-authored with Alun Gibbard.

From Plaid Cymru's viewpoint, they were much more organised in their campaign than I was. That was mainly because of the work of Peter Hughes Griffiths. He ensured that Plaid were more organised, with an improved strategy as well as revised electoral literature. By the time of the election Plaid workers, for example, had distributed a leaflet produced by Peter Hughes Griffiths to almost every house in the constituency. The leaflet *Gwynfor Evans and You* was effective. There was a full-page advertisement in the *Carmarthen Times* on 22 February, six days before the election.

The story in the Labour Party was very different. I had the same team, but four years older, the energy levels weren't what they used to be. Similarly, my energy levels were lower, partly because I had diverticulitis in the middle of the campaign. But more than that, because of my disillusionment that was emerging for my own party and specifically the opposition I had faced within the party on some subjects. There was also another key factor, both the Liberal and Conservative candidates were not as well known or of the same calibre as Huw Thomas and Lloyd Harvard Davies who contested the seat in 1970.

There was one unexpected debate right at the start of the campaign. The whole thing started just a few days before the election was called but lasted long after that. I was invited to be President of the Day at the National Eisteddfod in Carmarthen 1974. Plaid Cymru was furious. Peter Hughes Griffiths wrote an article in *Y Ddraig Goch* declaring his objection clearly and without mincing his words. Under the headline *Pam Gwynoro? (Why Gwynoro?)*, he doubts the wisdom of the Eisteddfod organisers in inviting someone so young. Usually, he said, they asked people who had made a lifelong contribution in some field or other, but I was only thirty years old. As part of the same debate, he said that the Eisteddfod had nothing to do with politics or sports. But there is a precedent for inviting Welsh-speaking Members of Parliament when the Eisteddfod is in their constituency to address the crowd – Jim Griffiths 1962, Ivor Davies 1964, John Morris 1966 and Gwynfor Evans himself in 1970. Each one of these within twelve years of the Carmarthen Eisteddfod.

He questioned the invitation because he didn't believe I had ever been a member of the Urdd, nor competed in any Eisteddfod. My objection to the ministers' stance was also a reason for me not to be a President of the Day as was the fact that I didn't have anything good to say about Cymdeithas yr Iaith – although of course, politics has nothing to do with the Eisteddfod, according to Peter Hughes Griffiths. He then said that I didn't use my Welsh and he hadn't seen anything that I had written in Welsh.

Unfortunately for him, the week his letter was published I had a Welsh article in one of Carmarthen's papers, one of many I had written over a period of years. I regularly contributed to television and radio programmes in Welsh. But there we are, another example of a very slack relationship between Plaid Cymru and real hard facts.

Naturally enough, the *Carmarthen Times* picked up on the story. In an editorial article, on 1 February 1974, the editor responded to Peter Hughes Griffiths's individual points and offered his own analysis. For example, on the point regarding my age, he draws attention to inconsistency in Peter's argument.

> *INCONSISTENCY NOTE: Later, Mr Hughes Griffiths listed eleven men who would have made a "worthier" choice. Among them are: Dafydd Iwan (hardly middle age) Tom Ellis, Labour MP (nothing to do with politics?) Barry John (nothing to do with rugby?)*

With regard to the point about writing in Welsh and the endless opportunities given to me to publish articles in the local newspaper, this is what the editor said, also referring to the fact that Peter said he was an ultra-Tory:

> *INCONSISTENCY NOTE: If the charge of ultra-Tory was correct, then why is "endless space" being allowed to Labour – or any other party for that matter?*

He summarised his argument by referring to the fact that an election was imminent.

... to attempt to publicly discredit the MP when his only "crime" is to accept an invitation from the National Eisteddfod committee to become a day president when the event is held in Carmarthen is not only untimely but thoroughly unworthy.

The Eisteddfod hadn't listened to Peter Hughes Griffiths, and I accepted the invitation to be the President of the Day on the Friday of the Eisteddfod. This whole matter was an example of the continued personal attacks on me. But, before the Eisteddfod, there was an election!

Night of the Count

I arrived at the count around midnight. The bookies still said that I was the favourite to win. But as I strode into the hall, my father and Dr Roger Thomas were waiting for me. They told me I was ahead by some eight votes. That strongly suggested that things would be very close.

The result of the count came at last and I was ahead by some ten votes. Gwynfor's team asked for a recount of the vote. The result of the recount was that I was ahead by four votes. Gwynfor called for another count. According to the third count, Gwynfor was ahead by four votes and naturally enough, I asked for the recount this time. By this time, it was six o'clock in the morning. There was quite a bit of excitement and tension, as you can imagine. A decision was made that it wouldn't be fair to undertake another count, eight hours after the counting team had started on their work the previous night. The count would restart at four o'clock Friday afternoon. There was a definite tension in the hall and amongst the crowd outside, and when the time of the count was announced, it intensified quite a bit.

Outside Carmarthen, the Labour Party had already suffered substantial losses – Elystan Morgan to Geraint Howells, for example and Goronwy Roberts and Wil Edwards to the two Dafydds from Plaid Cymru, Wigley and Elis Thomas. Throughout Britain, the situation between Heath and Wilson was also quite tight. Considering the wider context, everybody's eyes had turned on Carmarthen that Friday afternoon.

By half past seven that night, the result of the fourth count was that Gwynfor was ahead by only one vote. I asked for another count. But before the Returning Officer authorised that, they told the candidates that however close the next count would be, that would be the fifth and final count, and they would not authorise a sixth. Therefore, that was it. That would be the result.

They also announced that there would be a change in the counting method for the fifth time. This time, the candidates' votes would be counted one at a time, beginning with the one that was bottom of the previous count.

Bill Newton-Dunn, the Conservative, was announced first, 6,037 votes. Next was David Owen Jones, Liberal who was third, with 9,698. I was second and my vote was counted = same total as in the previous recount. I turned to my wife and said, "That's it, I've lost by one!"

Gwynfor's count was left. As that came to an end, one of the counters raised his hand and there were only forty-six votes in one bundle of fifty votes for Gwynfor. His majority of one turned to a majority of three for me.

Also, it became clear that ninety-seven voting papers

had been put to one side because there was no official pin mark on them which was necessary to make the ballot paper valid. So the party agents, but mainly agents for Gwynfor and myself, were holding papers up to the light to see if we could see any sign of official pinholes in them. That would be enough to make the voting paper valid. Some were accepted in this way. But Gwynfor had to make a personal point about this simple action. In his book *For the Sake of Wales,* this is what he said:

> *Poor old Gwynoro was on tenterhooks at the count... going over to the returning officer to inspect the slips that had been spoiled. He would hold one up against the light and examine it closely.*

Yes, I did do that, but for a reason. My dear friend, Ivor Morris, who had been with me from the start in 1967 and had been working for me untiringly in that election, was absolutely exhausted by the end of the count. He was in his seventies by then, so I did the work of checking the voting papers in his place.

The result stood. That was it. I had won. Once again Carmarthen had put drama and the unexpected into Welsh politics. I was back as a Member of Parliament for this tempestuous constituency – by three votes!

One version of that night's story that is on page three hundred and fifty of Rhys Evans's *Rhag Pob Brad* must be corrected. There, it says that Gwynfor had been under great pressure to call for a sixth count. It says he had wise advice from Wynne Samuel, who suggested it would be much better to lose by three votes than to win by such a thin majority. The Returning Officer, Gwilym Peregrine, had already called the candidates and their agents together to say that there would be no further count after the fifth; however close the result was. Suggesting that there was the possibility of a sixth in *Rhag Pob Brad* was not correct. It plays to the image of Gwynfor allowing things to happen, he wasn't losing, but giving his permission to lose.

On the point of what was best, winning by three or losing by three, I have often thought that perhaps it would have been better for me to lose by one rather than win by three. I then could have thrown my whole effort to canvassing over the coming months instead of being in Westminster week after week. But there was no guarantee that would have made a difference. Another way of looking at it was that at least I had an extra eight months in Parliament.

In the days that followed, there was quite a bit of speculation as to who the three were that ensured victory for me. Many came up to me to claim it was them, that it was their decision to go to vote with two friends late in the day that made the difference. Perhaps so, but I do know one thing: when I was sitting in the Labour Party office in Carmarthen, about nine o'clock on election night, Laura was out in the car still trying to gather votes whereas I had more or less given up. She went to the Park Hall Council estate in the town. In one house there were three elderly women all dressed in their night clothes. She managed to persuade them to come with her to vote, each putting an overcoat over their night clothes. I wonder if they were the three that made the difference after all. I would like to think so.

When I walked on the balcony to address the crowds after the announcement, I received a very fiery reception.

There was no way I could say a word, so loud was the noise coming from the hundreds below me. To be fair to him, Gwynfor asked the crowd to quieten and give me an opportunity to talk. I succeeded in saying a few words, and then I went back into the hall. We stayed there until the crowds dispersed and then walked the few hundred yards to our car. We were both glad that we succeeded in doing so this time, the complete opposite to 1970.

But we spoke too soon. When we arrived home, in Tanerdy, on the outskirts of Carmarthen, there was a police car there. Unknown to us, they had already been keeping an eye on the house for hours. The threatening telephone calls had started within less than an hour of announcing the result. Four in all, from different people, each one nasty and violent. They said that they knew where we lived and were watching my home. They had had enough of me and were determined to come for me.

Inside the house, the police told me that they would be listening to my telephone calls for a further three days and there would be a police presence outside the house over the weekend. It must be remembered that at the time, we had two small children under five years of age. I wondered if this was the result of Plaid Cymru not condemning violent behavior in the past.

Careful Consideration

Late on Friday and into the weekend, there wasn't a lack of analysis of the excitement of the result. Many had expected me to win comfortably. Then how did Plaid Cymru nearly win the seat back? That was the question. This is the answer offered by the *Carmarthen Journal*:

This is a most difficult question to answer but it might be that the people in the Carmarthen constituency, like in Scotland and elsewhere, are disillusioned with the big parties and were registering their protest.

The *Carmarthen Times* also contributed to the analysis:

Disillusioned with the two major parties because of their agricultural policies, local farmers (arguing that the Liberal candidate was young and untried) were openly saying that they were switching their allegiance to Plaid Cymru – as they did in the by-election in 1966.

To be completely honest, that hurt me quite a bit. I had done everything I could and everything that was asked of me for the NFU and the FUW.

On a much lighter level, several humorous stories raised their heads following the close result. I was told another example even as late as 2020, almost fifty years after the election. I was shopping in a local supermarket, and someone came up to talk to me. I didn't know him. He asked about my dog. This was a big surprise to me because, naturally enough, the dog was no longer with us. I asked how he knew about the dog. He said that he and his family had once put their dog in kennels in Llanedi, near Llanelli, whilst they went on holiday. Whilst they were away, there was much deliberation as to who they should vote for. After coming home, they went to get their pet. As they walked through the dog's home, he happened to pass this one dog's cage and it caught his eye. He saw that the dog's name was Gelert, as it was on the cage. He then noticed the owner's name, Gwynoro Jones. He turned to his wife and said that I was the one that would have their vote because my dog was in the same place as his. If this was true, and I have no reason to believe that it isn't, of course, then that was two of the three votes that proved to be so crucial for me! Having said that, over the years, I have heard many such stories, and the sum of votes of all these stories is much more than those three crucial votes. As far as I know, this is similar to everyone who insists that they were present at Stradey Park when Llanelli beat the All Blacks in 1972 – a total that is much more than Stradey Park could hold on any one occasion. But of course they are all correct.

The fervour of the election was also captured in song – believe it or not! A record was released by the Reverend Denzil Protheroe's son – I'm sorry, I can't remember the name of the group. It is still on YouTube today under the title *Cân Gwynoro*. Briefly, it makes light of me and mocks the majority of three. There are only four verses with the following chorus:

Pleidleiswyr bach Sir Gâr,
Peidiwch â dweud dim gair,
Os yw un yn fwy na digon,
Fi yw'r unig un â their.

In essence saying if a majority of one is enough I was the only one with three.

There was also reference to the former Prime Minister Harold Wilson in the song. With me meeting him on the way to "Number 10", Harold said to me:

Mae'r dyn cyffredin wrth y drws a ti sy nesa I fynd!

The ordinary man is at the door and you'll be the next to go!

One of the verses spoke about me meeting Leo Abse, and Leo said:

Wel, Gwynoro darling,
I fod yn safe MP,
Ma'n rhaid cael mwy nag ugain mil,
A nid y bloomin three.

To be a safe MP you need more than twenty thousand majority and not blooming three.

And this is how the song ended:

Mae Goronwy, Wil a 'Lystan wedi ffurfio grwp
I ennill bach o arian rol lando yn y swp.
Fe ganant 'Red Flag' weithie a hefyd 'Calon Lân
Ond pan yng ngwydd Gwynoro Jones...

This refers to Goronwy Roberts, Wil Edwards and Elystan Morgan who lost their seats in the February election, forming a music group to earn some money.

And then the chorus.

Years later, the song was one of my choices when I was a guest on *Beti a'i Phobol* on Radio Cymru. It is also on my YouTube channel today.

But whatever the amount of the majority, I had lived to

fight again. Back I went to Westminster on the Monday, but far from being certain that I would be there for as long a period as the first time.

Entering Parliament.

GOODBYE WESTMINSTER

After reaching Westminster, no Member of Parliament knew who would be forming the government of the day. Ted Heath tried his best to keep hold of his power as Prime Minister and succeeded – for a few days only. He tried to strike a bargain with Jeremy Thorpe, leader of the Liberals, which would keep him in power through a coalition. I believe that Thorpe was willing to come to an understanding with Heath to share power, but not so his Members of Parliament. Therefore, in light of no agreement, Harold Wilson became Prime Minister for the third time with a bare majority of three. At least I knew I was a Member of Parliament in a Labour government. But the situation was very fragile, and early on there was already talk of another election in the autumn. If that happened, it would have been the first time since 1910 for two elections to occur in the same year.

Gwynfor was right in his prediction. "If there was another election that year," he said, "Plaid Cymru would be in a stronger position than I would, and people would not be so simple as to think again that the Liberals would win a number of seats in Wales." Throughout the summer of 74, Gwynfor worked fervently to secure the favour of the Liberals and the Conservatives. From his point of view, that was the natural thing to do. But it must be said, that there was some degree of dishonesty in such a tactic as Plaid Cymru were moving more and more to the left at that time. From my point of view, there was no need for anyone to tell me how fragile a majority of three was.

As well as looking forward, I also wanted to look back. As was the norm for me, I wanted to analyse the result of the February election. It became clear that the Labour Party had received their lowest number of votes since 1935 in that election. A large number of Labour candidates had lost between 2,000 and 5,000 votes since 1970. In this respect, we did quite well in Carmarthen through only losing 1,600 on the 1970 vote. I was aware during the campaign that Labour's vote was weaker in some of its traditional strongholds with a degree of apathy and that was reflected in the turnout on polling day. Both the Liberal and Conservative vote fell by 1,000 each and Gwynfor seemed to have benefited from that with his vote increasing by just over 2,000. Across Wales it was a different story for the Liberals coming third, displacing Plaid Cymru from that position. The party's vote increased from 6% to 16% whilst Plaid Cymru's vote had dropped to 10%.

Greenhouses and Europe

Being a Prime Minister again gave Harold Wilson the opportunity to do something that Tom Ellis and I had suggested he should have done in January before the election. He had to replace George Thomas as Secretary of State for Wales. For a year and more prior to the election, George had caused great harm to the Labour Party in Wales. In his *Liverpool Daily Post* monthly column, he took every opportunity possible to disparage the Welsh language, culture and identity. I have no doubt that Labour lost votes in north and west Wales especially because of George's stance. He was creating divisions and causing damage. He just had to go.

Harold Wilson understood the problem and appointed John Morris as Secretary of State for Wales at the beginning of the new Parliament in March 1974. George wasn't happy at all; I tasted his displeasure shortly after that. I heard, through Cledwyn Hughes, that there was a possibility of me being promoted to a junior minister, either in the Ministry of Agriculture or Northern Ireland. Nothing came of it, and I heard later, from Fred Peart, the agriculture minister, that crucially George had poisoned my name with Harold Wilson.

Nevertheless an opportunity for new responsibilities came from two sources. I had a telephone call from Roy Jenkins who was Home Secretary asking me to be his Private Parliamentary Secretary. Often, receiving such an appointment was regarded as the first step towards being a minister. Some days later, I received a message from the Whip's office saying that I had been chosen as one of Parliament's UK delegation to the Council of Europe.

In May 1974, I went for a week to meet European Parliamentary Members in the European Council Assembly. I certainly created an impression there, in my first speech. I decided to open my very first contribution in Welsh. The seed was sown at dinner with John Smith the previous evening, who went on to become leader of the Labour Party.

As I stood on my feet, John whispered to me, "Do you want the standing ovation now or after?" When I started speaking, I could hear the translators in my ear announcing, "I think Mr Jones is speaking Welsh." This is how my speech opened:

I am grateful to you, Mr President, for allowing me to say a few words in my mother tongue in order to emphasise that this deputation from the United Kingdom represents three nations... Perhaps the Council would want to consider that I have spoken more Welsh in the European Council than I have in British Parliament.

In the press conference that followed, John Smith said, "...I think that it's a great thing he's done." But everyone was not of the same opinion. This is what David Rosser, Political Correspondent of the *Western Mail*, said in his weekly column:

That's not what some of his colleagues in Westminster are thinking.

Once again, I experienced the opposition of my fellow Labour Members of Parliament on the issue of the language. Things were made worse when the main British news programmes caught the story, giving it widespread publicity. When I phoned Laura to tell her what I had been doing, she already knew. More relevantly, the Labour officers in the constituency also knew and they were not at all happy. One of them had phoned Laura to ask why I had done such a thing.

It had been a continuous battle for me in my con-stituency, in the Labour Party and in Westminster to get people to understand that debating the case for devolution and cultural nationalism did not mean that I was a covert member of Plaid Cymru. In the constituency, the back-ground for this was completely clear. Since the beginning of the sixties, the battle between Labour and Gwynfor had been a fierce one, even on the County Council, where Gwynfor used to more often than not vote with the independent councillors. Therefore, it was very difficult for them to accept comments from me that sounded like what they had been battling against for such a long time. Everything that Plaid Cymru debated had to be fiercely opposed. Of course, I disagreed with quite a bit of Plaid's policies, but not on devolution, language and culture.

Speaking at Strasbourg.

155

At the end of my week in Strasbourg I was on the plane flying home. Before starting the flight whilst sitting on the plane, the pilot came out of his cabin to the passengers and asked if there was a Mr Jones amongst them. I raised my hand, and he came towards me with a bottle of champagne.

I come from Llanelli, and I've been flying this route for over twenty years. When I heard what you did in the Council you made me feel so proud!

At least someone understood and was appreciative.

Round about the same period, I was receiving regular messages about Gwynfor's market gardening business in Llangadog. Some of the workers were afraid that the business was having serious problems and as a result, they were afraid for their jobs. In order to avoid serious political repercussions should the business go completely bankrupt, Gwynfor's brother Alcwyn stepped in and kept the business going for a period, abating the effect of closure because of bankruptcy. One helpful result of this for Gwynfor was that he then had more time to fully involve himself in his political campaign.

My short period as Roy Jenkins's PPS wasn't without incident and controversy. 1974 was a period of intense Irish Republican Army activity. They bombed part of Parliament causing extensive damage and injuring eleven people and there were others including in Birmingham, Manchester and at the Tower of London. The Price sisters were jailed and an IRA prisoner died on hunger strike. For a period of two weeks in June a security alarm device linked to the police station in Carmarthen was placed at my home. I remember well one of the children set the alarm off and three police cars came racing to our house. The device did not stay long after that.

Then in July Roy Jenkins delivered a speech at a packed six-hundred-strong public meeting in Haverfordwest. I also spoke. It was widely regarded as the first shot indicating his displeasure in the leftward direction which he considered the Labour Party was moving.

Benn and Roger

Early in the 74 Parliament, I increasingly came face-to-face with the left-wing of the Labour Party. The climax was disagreeing publicly with Tony Benn, a figure who was increasingly influential and well-respected within sections of the Labour Party. By June, he had suggested a wide programme of nationalisation including land that could be developed for housing and industry. This was quickly seized upon by the other parties to claim that the Labour Party was "After Citizens' Land". It was very relevant in my constituency. My reaction was to say that such plans were irrelevant in the current political and economic climate. There were fears in the Labour Party that Tony Benn's influence was increasing and that Harold Wilson found it difficult to control him. I spoke at two full meetings of the Parliamentary Labour Party, saying that Benn's stance was causing electoral damage to Labour. I was listened to in silence. Then I released a statement which included this sentence.

The captain of the ship in the middle of a storm, does not attend a meeting called by his first mate to discuss the future direction of the voyage.

Everybody immediately understood that Wilson was the captain and Benn the first mate. I received an invitation for an interview on the ITN news programme, with Robert Kee interviewing me.

Gwynfor had latched on to some of Benn's comments and raised fears that Labour's intentions to put development land in public hands meant that farmland and gardens would be nationalised. Naturally enough, that raised real fears in Carmarthen.

For the second time within a short space of time, I was called to a meeting of the constituency Labour Party to explain myself. Some weeks after having to explain my Welsh speech in Brussels, I now had to explain my comments on Tony Benn. I succeeded in avoiding a reprimand on both occasions. The President of the constituency party, Dr. Roger Thomas, made one observation in the *Western Mail* on my comments on Benn:

I suspect that the left-wing element in the party could be upset by what was said but that perhaps is inevitable.

From February 74 onwards, Dr Roger Thomas was much more active with his writing of letters to the press. He regularly contributed to the *Western Mail*, for example. In looking back, it's clear that he had already started thinking about the next step in his political career. In one article, he compares the politics of the two Dafydds in Plaid Cymru with Gwynfor's politics.

On television the other night Dafydd Wigley reminded us that he and his fellow member had in the past three months supported the Labour government no fewer than on fifteen occasions with only three times against... Mr Evans, when he was our MP in 1966 – 1970, found himself able to support the Labour government on few and far between occasions... the two present members are so far left that they make Mr Evans appear to be the apotheosis of reactionary attitudes.

Devolution Heats Up

Without a doubt, the main topic of conversation in the summer and autumn of 74 was again devolution. The call for legislation on an Elected Council for Wales was increasing. Gwynfor was calling for a full-blown assembly within three years. Although I agreed with the principle, there was no way in the world that the timetable he suggested was realistic. But the government were taking big steps towards such a legislation. In the summer, two White Papers were announced, *Devolution within the United Kingdom: a Democracy* and *Devolution Proposals for Scotland and Wales*. There was another one to come in November, *Our Changing Democracy: Devolution to Scotland and Wales*. The Labour Party cannot be accused of not doing anything for Wales following the activities of that summer alone, but of course, Gwynfor was more than ready to do so. In an article, he said:

Every Labour voice which favours devolution and self-government has been silenced.

Palpably untrue and that after we had published two White Papers. I had emphasised many times that it is only a Labour government that would succeed in presenting legislation to create an Assembly for Wales. This was proved to be correct some twenty years later, with Gwynfor and I long gone from the political scene, and thirty years after the Carmarthen by-election, when Gwynfor and others prophesied that Wales would be independent within three years. This is what Dewi Watcyn Powell said when he was Chairman of Plaid Cymru's Constitutional Committee in 1969:

... that Plaid would have more MPs after the General Election, and the inauguration of a Welsh State by 1973 was possible.

In the *Guardian* on 23 September 1968, there was a report on Gwynfor's speech in his Party's Conference that year.

A prediction that Wales would be a one-party state for up to three years after independence came from the President. "Plaid Cymru will hold the reins of power for one, two, three years after self-government. By then, we have no doubt that other parties would have emerged, and we could contest elections."

He was suggesting a one-party dictatorship. Such comments were damaging to Plaid Cymru's political credibility. It was obvious to anyone who understood the system that such a thing was not practically possible; however right the principle was.

The Labour Party in Wales held a conference on the Kilbrandon Report. In my speech at the conference, I strongly debated the need to move quicker towards devolution, by establishing an Assembly with broad powers for Wales and equality with any legislation for Scotland. I quoted Lloyd George:

> *A generation that goes back on ground already gained doubles the march for its children.*

There was no need to guess who thought that he was responsible for any gaining of ground on devolution that happened at that time. Gwynfor was quite outspoken in speeches and conversations, saying that it was his victory in 66 that led to the Kilbrandon Commission and any discussion on devolution that followed on from that. Gwynfor claimed that in his party's conference in Aberystwyth, in the last week of October 1973. A report on his speech, which included vast quotations from it, was in the *Carmarthen Times* on 2 November, the day after publishing the Kilbrandon Report. This is what he said:

> *There would have been no Constitutional Commission but for Plaid Cymru. The process began with the Carmarthen by-election in 1966. It illustrates the truth that the way to get things done by government in Wales is through an independent national party.*

Naive at best. Such a sweeping statement ignores two central factors. Firstly, the key role of a nucleus of Welsh Labour Members of Parliament in the process of developing the Commission's report, and that on the back of campaigning within the party for years before that, on presenting devolution measures. People like Cledwyn Hughes were arguing such a case in the fifties, years before Gwynfor reached Westminster. In 1965, a year before Gwynfor won, a Working Party of the Welsh Labour Council called for establishing an Elected Council for Wales, a small step but an important one on the way to reforming the constitution of the British countries.

In 1968, the Labour Party established the Commission on the Constitution as a result of the discussions that had taken place for some years prior to that, when Gwynfor was a county councillor. In 1972 Parliament considered the Local Government Act that created new local authorities in Wales. I presented a motion to my Welsh Labour colleagues that would introduce an amendment to the Act calling for an Elected Council for Wales. The measure was supported by sixteen Welsh Labour Members of Parliament – Fred Evans, George Thomas, Donald Coleman, Brynmor John, John Morris, Cledwyn Hughes, Michael Foot, Denzil Davies, Tom Ellis, Caerwyn Roderick, Elystan Morgan, Gwilym Roberts, Wil Edwards, Neil McBride, A. Probert and me. At that exact time, perhaps it wasn't a full Assembly that was being offered by the sixteen, but a significant percentage of us wanted to see such a development.

The relevant point is, following Gwynfor's allegations, that calling for constitutional change was on the political agenda before 66. It is also interesting to note that Michael Foot's name was on the list. I persuaded him after two or three conversations to support the motion.

The second thing that Gwynfor ignored is quite simply Scotland. Alleging that it was the Carmarthen constituency that opened the door to devolution ignores the campaigning and the political pressure that came from Scotland before 66 to change the British constitution. The SNP were naturally a substantial power, but the weight of Labour's Scottish Members of Parliament was much stronger than our weight as Welsh Labour members. That was another indication of the "big me" by Gwynfor: saying that it was his victory that had changed everything in Britain.

Opening the Door

But on other matters, my disillusionment with the Labour Party was growing. The decision-making process, administrative structures and the unions' block vote gave me a headache. The climax came on 27 June 1974. I wrote to the Executive of the constituency Labour Party:

I cannot any longer conceal my acute concern about some developments in the Labour Party, which will not, in my view, enhance the prospects of the Labour Party and also affect the long-term unity of the Labour Movement. I happen to believe strongly in the principles of social democracy. Some doctrines which are propagated on the extreme left of the Labour party are neither cherished nor supported by the majority of those who vote Labour.

My colours had been nailed clearly and publicly on the mast. There were strong cries for me to be disciplined and for the Whip to be taken away from me. This time, the response not only came from the Party in Carmarthen, but nationally.

In his biography, Rhys Evans summarises my situation at the time.

Since about 1972, Gwynoro Jones had angered some of Labour's key players in the constituency with his support of Europe and his wariness towards the salary requests of the NUM. Worse than anything, from the point of the critics anyhow, was the fact that he sided with the right-wing of the Labour Party, that faction that included the heavy men such as Bill Rodgers and Roy Jenkins, the men who in seven years would establish the SDP. By the summer of 1974, the left-wing of the Labour Party wanted Gwynoro Jones' blood, and less loyal supporters started to withdraw. This happened to such a degree that Neil Kinnock, the member for Bedwellty and one of the left's most prominent speakers, could confidently allege that Gwynoro was a "... myopic old fool who, by denying the elementary conviction of the party has probably committed electoral hara-kiri – so we won't have to worry about him."

President of the Day

In the midst of such turmoil, it was good to have a break at the National Eisteddfod in Carmarthen in August 1974. I was to be President for the Day on the Friday, and that was a huge honour for me, and I was looking forward to it immensely. As a result, I worked on my speech for weeks, refining it, and each word was chosen carefully. I had learnt the speech and could say it from memory – something I was used to doing in my Sunday School days, learning verses etc. The press, because of the response earlier in the year when I first received the invitation, felt that there would be a warm welcome awaiting me. For example, the *Western Mail* correspondent:

> *With the festival motoring along in low key up until now, this is the afternoon everyone has been waiting for, and at 3pm, we were all packed into the pavilion to hear what he was going to say. The big question will be, "What will happen?" when the Labour MP for Carmarthen by three votes in the last election, steps up to the mike. Are the lads from Cymdeithas yr Iaith Gymraeg going to keep quiet, or is it all going to hit the fan?*

To be honest, I wasn't expecting any protesting, and there wasn't. I wrote a speech that showed my pride in my square mile and its culture. I noted the substantial contribution of a number of the county's residents to Welsh life, from Peter Williams to William Williams and Brinley Richards and Elfed.

> *We are very willing today to brag about what we do for the Welsh language, but friends, what about the efforts of the giants two centuries ago? These succeeded in publishing volumes in Welsh by the thousand without the help of a council, or government grant nor modern facilities to trade.*

I then referred to the mass media that were such a great part of our lives:

Certainly, our use of these media is defective – and especially the television. Therefore, when we have a Welsh Television Channel, and we are not going to take no for an answer, I am certain we will see it within two to three years, we must remember to make the best use of it. Yes, more Welsh programmes certainly, but what types of programmes? We need to raise the standards there.

The speech was received warmly. When I arrived home. I understood that it had all been televised, as my grandmother, who was confined to the house, had seen me. When I walked in through the door, she started to cry because that was the only time she had heard me making a speech. The subject of the speech was published in full in many of the local newspapers. My personal response was to consider whether the speech had done my election prospects any favours. I decided that it wasn't possible to know that, but at least I didn't think that I had done any harm to my cause.

The Door Closing

Some weeks later, on 18 September, Harold Wilson announced that there would be a General Election on 10 October. The last person for me to speak to in Westminster before I left for home for the campaigning was Dafydd Elis Thomas. He said to me, "You know that you're going to lose, don't you?" Without hesitation, I said, "Yes." He went on "...the Liberals and the Tories are going to vote tactically for Gwynfor and against Labour. Remember, I'm sorry but that's how it will be". I had the impression that there wasn't much love lost between Dafydd Êl and Gwynfor.

His observation reminded me of one made by the Chairman of the Labour Party in Wales, Ray Powell, who would be the Member of Parliament for Ogwr before long.

Look, Gwynoro, you might as well know that there are many of us in the Labour Party who are deeply unhappy with your stance on various party policies, and will be hoping that Gwynfor will win this election because it's best to cope with the enemy from the outside than the enemy inside the party.

I'm sure that there are no two quotes that summarise my situation better in 1974 than those from two so different as Dafydd Êl and Ray Powell.

The campaigning in October 1974 was as fervent as the campaigning in 1970, completely different to February. This was supposed to be a battle between two candidates only. Gwynfor and I spoke at a large number of meetings throughout the constituency, fifty-three in my case. The main subjects for discussion were devolution, the problems of the coal industry, plans for nationalisation by the Labour Party, and a few other subjects.

As at every other occasion, agriculture was a hot topic in the constituency. The Saturday following announcing the election, the NFU had a big protest through the centre of Carmarthen and then two public meetings in Pontargothi and Llanybydder. I was speaking at both meetings, as was Fred Peart, the agriculture minister. They were fiery meetings. I succeeded in addressing the farmers, but as I drove from there, I knew I had lost their vote despite having been their champion in Parliament for over four years.

Things weren't all a bed of roses for Gwynfor either. There were still divisions within Plaid Cymru and quite plainly, criticism on Gwynfor's style as leader of his party. For example, he was criticised for his one-eyed anti-Labour standpoint by Emyr Price.

> *Is it not a short-term policy, a policy that will eventually be counter-productive and unsuccessful, to rely on the dubious support of socio-esoteric factions that are anti-Labour and, in some cases, reactionary, rather than appealing to the breadth of the population – the normal working people.*

Rhys Evans places that particular observation in its wider context:

> *Gwynfor's fundamental problem was that the idea of a national movement that he was so fond of was an idea that was more suited to the Fifties and Sixties – an era when Plaid Cymru were looking for a foothold on the political ladder. Now, they have that foothold, and it needed more than the limited cultural agenda of a "national movement" if they want to escape from their Western chastisement.*

Therefore, we were both on shaky ground within our own parties.

On election night, the count was moved from the historic Town Hall to St Peters' Church Hall. Space for the public outside the front doors of the Hall was very limited, and quite soon tensions raised between supporters of both parties. The quick-thinking of Viv Fisher, the Chief Superintendent, succeeded in avoiding the tension from boiling over. His answer to conciliate the supporters was to start singing hymns and popular songs such as *Sosban Fach* and *Bendigedig fyddo'r Iesu*. It worked and succeeded in suppressing the over-enthusiastic crowd of some three thousand people.

The result of the election wasn't much of a surprise to anyone. The prediction beforehand was that Gwynfor would win and that the Liberal and Tory vote would collapse. Tactical voting happened in Carmarthen long before it became topical. Gwynfor's vote increased by 6,000. The Liberal vote fell by 4,300 votes and the Conservative one by 3,000. My vote increased by 2,500 from February 1974 and was a thousand higher than my vote in 1970 and I certainly took some comfort from that. At least, there were some that appreciated my efforts from 1970.

As could be expected, Gwynfor was over the moon and declared victoriously that the result in Carmarthen was a certain sign that Wales would have a Parliament before long. The sweeping statements were continuing.

There was one story from 1974 that has stayed with me until today. Before the elections, a local farmer had come to one of my surgeries. He had a huge growth on his nose, like an apple. It was obviously causing him and his wife much distress, and he had failed to get the health service to do anything about it. I promised that I would write to consultants at Glangwili hospital about his plight and concerns asking them to help him. That is what I did. I received a reply, promising that they would look into the matter further. Some weeks later, he came back to me to say that nothing had happened. I went to the hospital myself and asked to see one of the relevant doctors. I said that the whole thing was obviously placing the man and his family under a great strain and was a cause of great embarrassment to the farmer. I didn't hear a word after that. And then, after the October election, the front doorbell rang. It was the farmer with his wife, and his nose was perfectly healthy. He said that he wanted to thank me for arranging the treatment. He added that he didn't think that I should have lost the election because I deserved to win from the hard work I had done for the local people. This small story gave me a great deal of comfort when dealing with disappointment.

Aware for some weeks that it was going to be a difficult election I had seen an advertisement for a job, Director of Research and Information in Swansea for West Glamorgan Council. The closing date was the day after the election, so I sent for an application form in my father's name. I was that confident that I would lose the election, even though it was a disappointment when I did so. I had actually filled in the application form in the last week of the election and on the Friday morning drove to the Guildhall in Swansea to deliver it before the mid-day deadline. Thankfully, I got the job, so I was only out of work for some five weeks.

However in the period up to the end of the year I regularly looked back at what happened, especially in

1974 and in an address at a function organised by the Labour executive in Carmarthen I said:

One of the great personal advantages that has materialised since losing the election has been the opportunity to look at the political scene on a wider plane – free from the hurly-burly of political debate and realising that only through international cooperation can we pull through.

I freely confess that the last two months have been like a breath of fresh air.

One is now released from the intensity of seven years of political struggle and therefore freed from the constant danger of having to outflank and outbid the tactics and manoeuvrings of Plaid Cymru.

Any political candidate who has not had to contend with the tactics and operations of nationalists has not experienced the worse side of political struggles. One is always subjected to attempts at discrediting one's efforts … Over the last eight years important issues have been subjected to intense party-political jungle warfare… with bogus tactics as much based on innuendo and half-truths as on anything else … nationalists claiming credit for everything beneficial that was done.

Then their hero worship approach to politics with adulation and acclaim … whereas in fact much of what is being achieved is not down to one person but a community of people. It will always be a team effort and to claim otherwise is to do a grave disservice to the untiring efforts of many.

But my parliamentary career had come to an end.

TURNING THE TIDE OF TIME

Even though they were turbulent and exciting days, looking back to them has been very difficult at times. Evaluating a career is not something that you undertake lightly, especially as my own personal life comes under the magnifying glass in the process. I don't think we will see such a bitter period in Welsh politics again. Those were the days when members and supporters of Plaid Cymru and the Labour Party hated each other and refused to talk to each other, even when they lived in the same village, and that was throughout Wales, not only in Carmarthen. Many will find it difficult to believe that today. And such a political battle pivoted on Gwynfor's and my own personalities, two strong characters but so different, and that sets the scene of what I've had the opportunity to look back at in this volume.

There are things that I regret, without a doubt, and I will come to those shortly. But before that, how do I now look back at the other main character in this book, Gwynfor? How do I then look back at Plaid Cymru at that time? And of course, how do I consider my own party by now, the one I was a member of from 1960 until 1981, and a Member of Parliament in its name for over four years?

Gwynfor and I Now

Without a doubt, I said some quite harsh things about Gwynfor. And they needed saying. I do not regret those comments at all. It is difficult to believe today how much Gwynfor was idolised out of all reason, and that is a tendency that continues until today. There hasn't been a politician in Wales that was idolised by his followers as much as Gwynfor Evans. But he wasn't a god. As I have already said, he was far from being a good politician. He was an enthusiastic missionary at best. A very effective missionary, but that efficiency didn't make him a good politician at all. It is impossible to think of him in the same breath as some of the great politicians of the period, such as Clem Attlee, who transformed the Welfare State, Aneurin Bevan and the Health Service, Jim Griffiths the first Secretary of State for Wales, and before those three, Lloyd George. There are plenty more examples.

I felt I had to criticise him on his comments about Viet Nam; his unwillingness to condemn law-breaking and violence in the name of nationalism; the Second World War; his constant comparisons between Wales and political situations in other countries that had no relevance at all to his debate; the stance of the chapel ministers, and his never-ending disparaging of the Labour Party without ever condemning the Tories – all these points, and many others, deserved to be criticised because they were a combination of being incorrect, misleading, superficial and naïve.

At the time, I hadn't seen many personal qualities to admire in Gwynfor himself. But the passage of the years has enabled me to see things differently. It's clear to me now that he had positive personal qualities. The most pre-dominant of those was his perseverance. For example, he succeeded in fighting against the Labour Party machine, more often than not, on his own. And that for a long period of time. He had a vision, formed his vision and kept at it; I'm sure that if he was alive today, we would agree on several things in the context of the future of Wales as a nation.

It is worth noting that in those eight years both of us were fighting against each other, we only spoke face-to-face for less than five minutes. There was obvious antipathy and an element of hatred between the two of us and neither of us respected the other. I'm sure that I was the one that showed it most outwardly. It became clear that Gwynfor kept his comments about me for his conversations with his friends and for his writing. He ensured that it was others who wrote to the press and fired the bullets on his behalf. But this was a battle between two personalities that fired the central direction of the politics of the whole of Wales for the period.

I shall come back to his wider political vision later. At best, they were impractical dreams. It was political and logical nonsense to allege so confidently on several occasions that Wales would have its own government within three years after he won the by-election in 1966 and especially after regaining his seat in October 1974. It was foolishness to say that such a Wales would be a one-party nation in the early years. The reality of it was that it took over thirty years after Gwynfor's victory in 66, before the Welsh Assembly was established. It called for a wiser and more realistic strategy on Gwynfor's part, and things would have been very different had he been able to understand that.

At the time, Wales, and the rest of the British countries,

were united by the heavy industries, particularly coal and steel. Institutions throughout Britain were controlling such industries, unions and managers. There is no need for a clearer example than the British Coal Board and the NUM. There was something that united the workers of the South Wales Coalfield with workers in the English and Scottish coalfields. This union was beyond any other consideration. It would be futile and foolish to fight a self-government battle against such a backdrop. It called for a different type of vision and strategies, such as those drawn up by the Kilbrandon Commission.

It must be acknowledged that many had a role in the process that led to the National Assembly that was established in 1999 and it is time to rectify the misleading and erroneous impression created over the years, that it was only Plaid Cymru that gave us devolution and the status to the language. In this respect, there was nobody worse than Gwynfor himself for creating such an impression. The records of several Liberal, Labour, and even to some extent Conservative governments since the 1880s reveal that they contributed substantially to aspects of devolution and status for the Welsh language, and that they did so without much influence from Plaid Cymru. Gwynfor's eagerness to claim the praise for every constitutional development also ignores the substantially larger contribution from the SNP in Scotland.

Plaid Cymru at That Time

As Gwynfor held so stubbornly tight to his attacks on the Labour Party, refusing to even mention the Tories, Plaid moved to be the party for the Welsh-speaking Welsh people of the west – Carmarthen, Meirionnydd and Caernarfon were the only electoral targets important to him whilst many in his party were stressing the equal importance of the south Wales valleys – with constituencies such as Caerphilly, Rhondda and Merthyr.

It made it impossible for the Labour Party to see any virtue in what he or his party were also doing because of the intensity of his attacks. Had he been cleverer and more astute, he would have succeeded in attracting some of the Labour Party members to walk side by side with him to recognise the individual contributions of Plaid Cymru. Through that, it is possible he would have gained some ground, even if that had only been on the margins. What happened in the by-elections in the late 1960s was testimony to that. But whilst he was blindly attacking the Labour Party, there was no hope of any level of cooperation and joint working as there is now. Did he genuinely expect the Labour Party to respond to his requests whilst he was disparaging them at every opportunity possible and for such a long time? That was a completely naïve political stance attitude that showed that he wasn't a natural politician in the first place.

Putting these observations down on paper made me consider where Gwynfor would be in the Plaid Cymru that we have today. I am not so sure as to what sort of role Gwynfor would have found in a Plaid Cymru that was led by Leanne Wood or later Adam Price. There is no room for the *Pethe,* the cultural considerations, in their politics. Not that either were unaware of the Welsh culture. Yet, it was not the heartbeat of their strategy and political policies, as was the case for so many Plaid members during the period under review in this book. It is true however that Leanne and Adam's differing emphases has led to Plaid extending its appeal and widening its electoral success but nothing near to what they had expected. The leftward lurch has not delivered sufficient meaningful success in the south Wales valleys and that is no surprise. I am of the belief that by today, Gwynfor would probably have distanced himself from the party just as his predecessor Saunders Lewis had.

The Big 'I'

This brings me to the biggest change that has happened when preparing this book. It involves defining the central element of political nationalism. In that context, we've heard quite a lot about Independence over the last few years. An independent Wales is the slogan. That was Leanne Wood's chorus to some extent, but it was even more so for her successor, Adam Price. But this is a relatively new song for Plaid Cymru. Throughout the eighties and well into the 2010s, Plaid Cymru was very quiet on self-government for Wales, let alone independence. The truth is that it is the Yes Cymru movement that has eventually awakened Plaid Cymru from its slumber on the issue.

But, from which hymn book was Gwynfor singing? The evaluation, the scrutiny and analysis in preparation for this book and reading twenty years of Plaid Cymru executive minutes from the 1960s to the 1980s, clearly shows that his hands, nor indeed Plaid Cymru's, weren't holding the same hymn sheet. He was closer to his predecessor, Saunders Lewis, who spoke in terms of dominion status, and after that, Gwynfor spoke in terms of confederalism in the 1980s. Independence was not part of the vocabulary of either of the two.

Plaid's two early leaders never used the word independence at all. *The Story of Saunders Lewis* by Gwynn ap Gwilym 2011, notes a comment made by Saunders Lewis in 1926.

> *Do not ask for independence for Wales. Not because it is impracticable but because it's not worth having... we want not independence but freedom and the meaning of freedom in this respect is responsibility. We who are Welsh claim that we are responsible for civilisation and social life in our part of Europe.*

Gwynn ap Gwilym argued further:

> *The National Party's aim was "Dominion Status" under British Sovereignty... and that its true ideal was for Wales to be one of a league of equal European states.*

It's worth noting that Saunders Lewis was to some extent a visionary. He wrote about an equal league of European states in 1926, over thirty years before the European Economic Community was created and half a century before Britain joined the European Economic Community. He considered independence impractical and because of that, not worth having. In 1975, in a lecture on "The Principles of Nationalism", he repeated what he had said in 1926. *"Independence is a material debate and there are higher principles than only material ones".*

A year later, in 1976, Pennar Davies published a book

on Gwynfor, *Gwynfor Evans, His work and Thoughts*. In it he summarised his understanding of Gwynfor's viewpoint:

> ... it is not independence in the form of "untarnished sovereignty" that is Plaid Cymru's aim but an essential freedom to co-operate and work with other nations.

There was further evaluation of that stance in Rhys Evans's biography of Gwynfor. Here's an excerpt from the book that summarises it quite clearly:

> A further error on Gwynfor's part was for him to publish a leaflet that transformed Plaid Cymru's constitutional policy without consulting with anybody. "Self-government for Wales and a Common Market for the Nations of Britain" was published in order to attract members of the Labour Party and kill the accusation that self-government would be a disaster. From there on, Gwynfor hoped to see a Common Market that was based on the countries of the British Isles. The clear intent was to bury the idea that Plaid Cymru wanted to "cut Wales's economic life away from England" but in doing so, the policy for dominion status was also buried in one blow. In its place, Plaid Cymru started to call for Commonwealth status. Gwynfor's intention was to set Plaid Cymru's constitutional aims within a modern context, but for the purist nationalists this was further evidence that the party had jumped on the "free trade bandwagon".
>
> In private, some of the more independent members of the Working Party were much more damning. For

example, Harri Webb believed that the whole talk about a British Customs Union was foolery, and that the new idea reflected the train of thought of a party that was full of "docile decorous language nationalists". Plaid Cymru's attitude towards the Welsh language and the best way of protecting it, was also central to this discussion about the future of the party and its president.

After the 1960 annual conference, it was seen that the younger members of the Party were more and more judgemental about the way forward, and with Gwynfor so barren the space was filled by their observations. This was also the opinion of those civil servants who kept an eye on Wales. In October 1960, Blaise Gillie wrote to Henry Brooke to warn him that there was a: "... widespread impression that Alderman Gwynfor Evans, the present leader of the Party, is in danger of losing his grip over the party to an extreme and younger section."

Gwynfor Evans:
A Portrait of a Patriot, Rhys Evans, Lolfa 2008

One question came back to mind regularly over the years. If Gwynfor wasn't completely convinced about independence, why didn't he make that point clear in his political campaigning between 1966 and 1974? Why did he choose to accept the comments, the allegations, about Plaid Cymru's stand on independence and referred to all the time as "separatists" without questioning or challenging them? It was only in the 1980s that it became clear that independence was not his aim, but more of a confederal Britain with its own common market. The problem he had was that a strong and influential group inside the executive and the wider party did want separation from England so he had to walk a fine line.

The party's evidence to the Independent Commission on the Constitutional Future of Wales *The Road to Independence* published in book form in 2022 emphasises the potential of a confederal future. Claiming that the party has long favoured a confederal approach citing that in 1982 Gwynfor Evans in his publication *The End of Britishness* had made the case for such a constitutional arrangement.

I recall commenting about this on one of my social websites. I received quite an unexpected response. Amongst the favourable comments to what I had written, one came from Gwynfor's grandson, Mabon (who is now a prominent Plaid Senedd member). His comment, quite simply, was to say that his grandfather hadn't spoken about independence. That confirmed my understanding of the situation during the period being reviewed by this book. Although I had no memory or comprehension of Gwynfor having used the term "independence", neither do I remember Gwynfor denouncing the term in his speeches, interviews and newspaper articles during the period in question. Had he done so, it would have alleviated and lightened the bitterness and conflict between us considerably.

It would also have pulled Gwynfor and I much closer together than we had ever been politically and perhaps very possibly personally as well. That is a point I have often mused over, wondering where it would have led us.

Different brushstrokes

As the Seventies unfolded, within my own party, there was a clear feeling that they felt a need to put a stop on the young Member for Carmarthen because he was far too willing to speak his mind. I didn't have much patience towards a number of prominent members of my own party, especially the ones on the extreme left-wing that were, in my opinion, completely unrealistic and promoting policies that I couldn't agree with. But for me, the most important point in this context is that there were too many Labour members of parliament, Labour councillors and ordinary party members who were so clearly anti-Welsh in their whole being or at best agnostic towards all things Welsh in their stance and utterances, and I found it very difficult to accept and process that. That was a key l factor as to why I was so unhappy in the party. It created tension and hurt for me personally. I was born, naturally, a Labour boy but I found it difficult to countenance how people with such opinions could be a part of the same party as me. We didn't remotely think about Wales in the same way.

But the atmosphere that prevailed in the 60s and 70s has changed beyond recognition. There is more interaction and cooperation between Labour and Plaid Cymru members over the last decade or so than was ever dreamt possible in the last century. The two parties have learnt that there is a way to disagree, hold different viewpoints, without having to engage in vitriol and hatred as existed decades ago.

Plaid Cymru and Welsh Labour have worked together in the Senedd for the best part of fifteen years or so, even forming in coalition government together. Even twenty years ago that would have been unthinkable and anathema to the supporters of both parties.

Returning to my personal experience, that is what was true of myself and the people from the village of my birth, Foelgastell and also the village next door, Cefneithin, when I was a child and a young man. It was completely natural for me to go to the homes of Jac, from the duo Jac a Wil, D.H. Culpitt the bard and Wil Rees y Brwshys; the three were staunch Plaid men. But I was severely criticised by the Labour Party for communicating with these three, just as the three were judged by Plaid Cymru for speaking with me.

In 1976 Dai Culpitt composed a poem on my endeavours as a Member of Parliament and it brought some negative reaction from members of Plaid Cymru. One I recall was by the well-known and successful Welsh language poet Alan Llwyd who disliked the reference to "the crowds spreading laurels beneath your feet". Some local Labour party activists were upset by the reference to "crucified by the same old crew". This is the poem roughly translated:

It's true we weren't from the same political party
But every man is free to choose his faith and opinion
You wandered eagerly around the parliamentary floor
Demolishing all the old prejudices
You perspired a lot for your beliefs
And turned every stone for what was right
You were very industrious, not taking a break
Achieved to fill your working day
You rode like Him on a white mule

With the crowd spreading laurels beneath your feet
They then endlessly sang your praises
Although some were baying for your blood
But you were crucified by the same old crew
That shouted "Hosanna" on the way to Jeriw!

The spirit of Foelgastell and Cefneithin is to be seen today. At the early rallies for Yes Cymru in 2016/17 I met up with members of Gwynfor's family – his daughter Meinir, who was in prison during the time her father and I were battling with each other, and Hedd Gwynfor. Back in the 70s I said that Gwynfor was more than ready to accompany language protestors to the prison door only to leave them and return to the comfort of his home. So, I found it personally pleasing that we were able to talk to each other amicably in a way that wouldn't have been possible during the period this book covers. I must say, that is a great comfort to me.

Leaving Labour

In the second part of the Seventies, Roy Jenkins became the President of the European Commission. I kept in close contact with him over a period of four years, through regular letters, until he finished in 1980. And because of this letter writing, I knew in 1978 that it was more than likely that on his return from Brussels a new party would be formed, and I supported and encouraged Roy Jenkins to do so.

It was no surprise, therefore, for me to leave Labour at the beginning of the Eighties when the new SDP party was formed. I joined its founders, Roy Jenkins, David Owen,

Shirley Williams, Bill Rodgers and others, to offer a new answer for the people of Britain. On the matter of devolution and a federal Britain, this was a new fascinating episode. I had more opportunity to speak and promote the subject and to debate its cause than I ever had in the Labour Party, and this was on a British level. I made speeches on devolution throughout Britain. Throughout most of the Eighties, I was Chairman of the SDP in Wales, co-chairman with Winston Roddick from the Alliance between the SDP and the Liberals, and I was also on the SDP's UK National Committee and, after that, on the Liberal Democrat's one as well. Through these various responsibilities, I had influence on a much wider span of policies than the influence I had on devolution alone within the Labour Party. On two specific occasions, this meant standing against one of the founders of the SDP, David Owen, who was against devolution at the time. I won an internal vote against him, and the party, as a result, supporting devolution. I am very proud of that.

Without a doubt, in the Eighties, the SDP were more forward-thinking than any other party, in calling for devolution. Plaid Cymru, and even Gwynfor and the leaders who followed him, Dafydd Elis Thomas and Dafydd Wigley, went very quiet on the subject during that decade. Indeed, even for the twenty years between 1997 and 2017. Here is a taste of what I said:

The word "independence" was used about 150 times by the SNP in Scotland in electoral manifestos and other publications during that period but only 115 times by Plaid Cymru. It would be unfair to place all the blame on Gwynfor. The no turning back fact is, if it wasn't for Scottish politics in the nineties and Blair's government after that, devolution would not have taken place. Scotland was central to British politics in those days. Blair understood that he had to react to that. Devolution had been a stumbling block in Britain for a quarter of a century and more before that. Even though Wilson created the Welsh Office etc., it was vital that you had a Prime Minister who believed in that matter. Whatever his motives for doing so, Blair accepted the need for devolution. In Wales, that was during a period when the majority of Labour party members in the country didn't want devolution.

The SDP and the Liberal Democrats were strong advocates of reforming the voting system, calling for a written constitution, a federal Britain, an elected second chamber to replace the House of Lords and of course strong adherence to being part of the European Community. Here we are decades after and those remain live issues.

Independence today

I have argued the cause of devolution for Wales since the Sixties. Nothing has changed. Wales's situation has changed considerably of course, as has its economy. I have already referred to the destruction of the British institutions that were uniting the countries of Britain via heavy industries and strong trade unions. Coal was king in each of Britain's countries, as was steel. Those industries and organisations are long gone and even as I conclude we witness the uncertainity of the Port Talbot steel works complex.

Today, the reality of the situation is that seven of the countries that are members of the European Union have a population which is less than that of Wales, and their money per head of the population is less than Wales also. To me, the traditional debate, "Can Wales afford it?" has long gone because of that. Wales can be a sovereign country that governs itself. I am not over fond of the word independence – like Saunders Lewis and Gwynfor – but how to reach the aim is the big task now. The future belongs to a federal or confederal Britain – although I fear it could be a decade or two before any of it materialises. Fact is that there are powerful forces at work determined to retain as far as is possible a centralised system of governing Britain. Any reform is seen as a major threat. These forces reside in the two-bid parties, the civil service, financial and industrial organisations, the media and wider afield.

That is why there is still the need for fervent campaigning as Yes Cymru are doing and it was a major step forward that the Welsh Government set up its own Independent Constitutional Commission on the future governance of Wales. That Commission's findings will provide a lot of food for thought but I fear that it will not move us much further forward than raising the usual options that will be debated upon for years to come. Unfortunately, it is the nature of politics as far as governing Wales and Britain goes – yes, too many powerful forces at work against reform.

The likelihood is that there will be a Labour government sometime in 2024 and if it does not radically move the dial forward over the next decade then pretty much the status quo will prevail other than tinkering with the edges of greater devolutionary powers under existing structures. In my bones I fear that the omens are not good for radical reform.

Family matters

Before concluding, I must acknowledge the contribution of my former wife Laura to my political campaigning during those Carmarthen years. I spoke earlier of her untiring campaigning on my behalf before the 1970 Election and also both elections in 1974. Also, when I was a Member of Parliament, and up in London with my work, Laura would represent me in meetings and events back in the constituency. Remembering that she had two children under the age of five to bring up so often on her own.

Indeed, she was the one responsible for sparking an awareness of Plaid Cymru people in me. She used to be a member of Young Plaid Cymru, under the influence of the community where she was brought up, namely Garnswllt, near Ammanford. In the same chapel as her was Ieuan Wyn Jones, the one who became a Member of Parliament for Plaid Cymru, and his brother Rhisiart Arwel. I have a clear memory of a book that Laura had when we first met. Unfortunately, I don't remember the title, but I do remember the picture on the cover. It was a picture of a cow with her body in England but she was eating Welsh grass. Such a book created quite a storm. The impression it created on me personally was completely clear. I remember asking myself, "Why is it like this?"

Laura and I were deeply disappointed. We had given our all to the constituency, fought for every section of people, communities and businesses within it. I was active in Parliament and was making an impact. But it was all killed off by tactical voting to stop Labour by the Conservatives and Liberal voters.

We remained in Tanerdy until the early part of 1975 when we moved to West Cross in Swansea. It wasn't just the travelling every day, we just needed to be away from the scene and environment that had ended in such a disappointment. Also 1974 had been a very stressful year – politics impacts not just on adults but children too, who are more aware than is realised of political ill feeling and ill will. I had been working for West Glamorgan County Council in Swansea as Director of Research and Information for some months by then. My intention was to stand again in Carmarthen and the next General Election but it did not work out – and that was my fault. That was a big mistake.

As I was living in Swansea, I was on the periphery, with regard to the Labour Party's activities in the Carmarthen constituency, and there had been no contact between us for two years and more. My political life was engaged in the Swansea Labour Association and the Sketty ward. However in 1977 I received a letter inviting me to offer my name as a candidate for the General Election in Carmarthen, and I did so. I understood afterwards, by word from other people some weeks later, that Dr Roger Thomas had also entered his name. I was somewhat disappointed that he hadn't told me himself of his interest, as we were close friends in those years. When the nomination process was finished, I received seventeen nominations from Labour Party branches in the constituency, as well as from local unions. Roger only had four nominations. I had a comfortable majority. That strongly suggested that I would have succeeded in being chosen. But that's not what happened.

It became clear to me that the officers of the executive, who were different to the ones that I had with me in 1967-74, were very supportive of Roger. As a result, they were doing everything they could to push Roger forward, regardless of the nomination count. To me, that endangered the unity that there had been in the constituency party for the best part of eight years. My response then was to withdraw my name even though they implored me not to do so. That opened the door for Roger Thomas. When voting day came in the 1979 General Election, Roger won, beating Gwynfor. That was a bad day for me sitting in my office in County Hall Swansea.

Roger did explain in an interview with the editor of the *Carmarthen Times* why he thought I was out of step with the constituency party:

> *With hindsight I suppose that Gwynoro's switch from a vociferous anti-Marketeer to such an out and out pro-Marketeer upset some in the party... For Gwynoro, accepting the post as Roy Jenkins's PPS was in addition to being an honour, a calculated risk. Now his views on all topics were more apparent, his position in the political spectrum (I assume Roger meant as a social democrat) settled for all, including Unions and individuals opposed to the Market, to digest.*

My response was, without a doubt, naïve and immature. I should have accepted that a contest with Roger was going to take place and follow the view of the majority of the membership that was supporting me and stood against Gwynfor once again.

I often think about what the result would have been had I stood, thereby resurrecting the old enmity between Gwynfor and myself. It's possible I would have won, as Roger did. After all, that year the Tories were extremely popular, and Conservatives voters in the Carmarthen constituency returned to the fold and moved their votes back to their own party instead of supporting Gwynfor. Liberals did likewise. The massive tactical voting of October 1974 had been abandoned and party allegiances returned to how it was in 1970. But at other times, I doubt whether I would have won because the battle between Gwynfor and I would have been very different to the one that took place between Roger and Gwynfor; no one will know how things would have gone.

There was another factor that guided my decision not to stand and that was a family one. By 1977 we had three children all under the age of nine. The commitment to campaigning weekend in weekend out that I gave for three years 1967-70 was going to be impossible.

It is but a ghost that whispers in my ear, "What if..." What if I had stood in 1979 in Carmarthen? What if I had remained in the Labour Party? Obviously with the passage of the decades and all the new opportunities that came my way in education and business, such questions have faded into the ether.

At such times, it is my children's words that comfort me. The three, Glyndwr Cennydd, Indeg and Penri, have experienced very successful careers in their chosen fields

– Chief Executive, Solicitor and International Director. I am very proud of them. On several occasions, independently of each other, when they hear me whispering, "What if ...?" they say to me, "If you had been offered the life you had when you were a child, would you have accepted it?" My unwavering answer each time is that I would have quite happily accepted it. Even so, I still strongly believe that I would have achieved much more if I had stayed in politics after 1992. One big disappointment was for me to miss the opportunity to be a member of the Senedd in Cardiff.

I am very glad that I have been able to have been part of one of the most dramatic periods in the history of Welsh politics. These days my political enthusiasm and passion comes to the fore on social media. It is strange how political circumstances and viewpoints today are so very similar to the period of political battle I have recalled in these pages. It is even more strange when you consider how the nature of politics today suggests that Gwynfor and I would have been much closer than the events of Carmarthen in the late Sixties and early Seventies suggest. If only the two of us had spoken to each other...

Mr Gwynoro Jones, Mr Gwilym Peregrine a Mr Gwynfor Evans wedi oriau o ddisgwyl am ganlyniad hanesyddol Caerfyrddin.

At the count, Gwynoro, Gwynfor and Returning Officer.

A RATHER SPECIAL BOXING CONTEST

Gwilym Owen

First written for the Welsh language edition
Gwynoro a Gwynfor (Lolfa 2019)

GWYNORO a GWYNFOR. When I first saw the title of this volume, I imagined that I was looking at a poster hyping up a rather special boxing contest. Indeed, after much consideration, I must admit that I wasn't far from it. What Gwynoro Jones and Alun Gibbard have achieved is to chronicle a massive political battle in one Welsh constituency. A battle which lasted for eight years between 1966 and 1974, even though it was only once or twice that the two boxers themselves ever met face-to-face.

In one corner, you have Gwynfor Evans, a highly respected businessman, President of Plaid Cymru, County Councillor in Carmarthenshire, Treasurer for the Union of Welsh Independents, and above all, the man who had succeeded in delivering quite a blow to the Labour Party in a historic by-election following the sudden death of Lady Megan Lloyd George. And he was the Member of Parliament for Carmarthen. Plaid Cymru's first representative in Westminster.

In the other corner is Gwynoro Jones, a native of the Gwendraeth Valley, who was twenty-four years old when he succeeded in beating two other candidates in the race for the nomination to be the Labour Party candidate. And as a Lay Preacher, he had close links with the religious life of the constituency.

From the beginning, there wasn't much brotherly love between the two, as individuals or between their parties. Almost daily, an atmosphere of personal ridicule and satire, bitterness and bickering could be seen. Indeed, it could be claimed that antipathy existed at every level. And as a journalist who worked as a reporter, presenter and editor on political programmes for TWW (what is TWW?) and HTV Wales during that period, I can testify that such an atmosphere was unique in the history of Welsh politics.

What is particularly interesting about this book is how the authors have gathered the material for the commentary on the big fight. Of course, there were all sorts of speeches and meetings to be considered. There was some radio and television. But most of Gwynoro Jones and Gwynfor Evans's politicising at that time took place in the pages of the local newspapers, namely the *Carmarthen Times*, the *Carmarthen Journal* and the *Guardian*, and the *Western Mail* and the *Evening Post*. In the columns of these papers, the two boxers and their supporters would wallop each other relentlessly with articles and letters. Alun Gibbard is to be congratulated on his research and analysis of this troubled and interesting period in the political history of Carmarthen.

Of course, there are peaks to the story. The first is Gwynoro's victory in the 1970 Election which gave him four years in Westminster. Then going back for a few months following his hair's breadth victory in the first Election of 1974. And then, the finale, the second Election in 1974. This time, it was Gwynoro's turn to receive a punch from Gwynfor. Although perhaps the Labourites in the Gwendraeth Valley might regret it he decided not to come back for another contest in 1979. Gwynfor would lose that bout, but to a different Labour candidate.

In the Sixties and Seventies of the last century, foundations were laid which made it possible for Welsh politics to stride towards the independence that is gradually developing in Cardiff Bay. And certainly, a crucial part of that story can be found on the pages of this volume.

Gwilym Owen
March 2019

Gwilym Owen was former head of news and current affairs at HTV and BBC Wales. He died July 2019. This commentary was first published in the Welsh language version *Gwynoro a Gwynfor* (Y Lolfa 2019) as a preface.

GWYNORO JONES

Your Labour Candidate says:

THIS GENERAL Election will decide which of two parties will form the next Government. There is only one alternative to Labour — and another Conservative Government would be disastrous for Wales and this constituency.

The new foundations of a New Wales is being laid by Labour, although the job has not yet been completed. A start has been made and responsible opinion suggests that the 70's will be the years of growth. The national "Times" said in March, 1969, of Wales:

"There are facts and solid achievements to justify the feeling that a decade of growth lies ahead".

Then Professor Brinley Thomas in January said:

"Whatever our professional purveyors of gloom may say, the economic prospects for Wales in the seventies are distinctly favourable."

It is important that the people of this constituency do not opt out of this choice. Can we really afford another Conservative Government that built only 11 advanced factories in 13 years; spent only £1m. in 1964 on Welsh industry; built no health centre in 13 years; is prepared to dismantle Labour's Development Area Policy?

Despite all the difficulties the Government's record in the social services — housing, health and welfare, education, pensions, social security is one of tremendous achievement.

Mae Llafur yn parhau i fod yn gyfaill da i Gymru, ac byddai y dyfodol yn ansicr iawn pe bai y Toriaid yn llywodraethu eto. Llafur yn unig o'r ddwy blaid fawr sydd wedi cydnabod pwysigrwydd Cymru a'i chymeryd fel cenedl.

EICH YMGEISYDD LLAFUR

Better roads for the 70s

THANKS to Labour, and as a result of the creation of the office of Secretary of State, Wales's road network will be transformed in the 1970's. No longer will we have to suffer as a result of Conservative neglect from 1951-64.

The Carmarthen constituency will benefit immensely from the new road plans.

Gwynoro Jones, your Labour candidate, outlined in a report on the constituency well over a year ago the needs of Carmarthen, calling for major road improvements.

Now we know that Labour's programme will mean:

Motorway from London to Swansea by 1976. A dual carriageway from Carmarthen to St. Clears. A by-pass of Carmarthen, as well as Cross Hands, Dryslwn and St. Clears. Second Bridge over the Tywi.

Already under construction is a 1-mile diversion of Carmarthen costing £1m. and a by-pass of Llanwrda.

There is also the need to improve the road between Abergavenny and Carmarthen and the town of Llandeilo merits special attention.

The by-pass of Morriston and Pontardulais will also aid the development and prosperity of our constituency.

GWYNORO JONES SAYS:

"The improvements and plans are due to the work of a Labour Government. If only the Tories had planned an adequate road programme when in office. Don't let them destroy the plans for the 70's."

HOUSING SUCCESS

IN THE last five years well over 95,000 houses have been completed in Wales — an average of more than 19,000 per year.

In 1967, a record total of 20,000 was achieved. This compares with the Tories "achievement" from 1960 of only 72,500.

Labour has increased the building rate by 25 per cent.

Canolfannau Iechyd

Ni adeiladodd y Toriaid un Canolfan Iechyd yng Nghymru mewn 13 o flynyddoedd.

Mae Llafur yn barod wedi adeiladu 18 ac mae pymtheg yn rhagor yn cael ei hadeiladu.

In five years, Labour has built 14,000 local authority houses more than the Tories did from 1960 to 1964. Neither have they neglected the private sector. A record number of private houses were built, almost 10,000 more than the Tories over the five year period.

In 1969, there was a slight drop in the overall number of houses completed. The figure was 1,800 below the previous year but still 3,300 greater than the number completed in 1963, the last full year of Tory rule.

Election special leaflet.

WHAT I SAW, HEARD AND TESTIFIED

When *Gwynoro a Gwynfor* was published almost fifty years had gone by. That is a very long time in politics. Most certainly the Wales of these days is far removed from the 1960-80s when both of us were fully engaged in the politics of our nation. The relationship between Plaid Cymru and Labour is far more tranquil since the establishment of the Senedd compared to the turbulence of decades past.

Gwynoro a Gwynfor was first published in 2019 by Y Lolfa. Ever since then I have been asked if an English-language version would be available in due course. It has taken some time. Alun and I have written two other books – *Whose Wales? The Battle for Welsh devolution and nationhood 1880-2020* and the other being *The Forgotten Decade: Political Upheaval and Industrial Strife in 1980s Wales*.

But I believe it's appropriate that an account of those times should now coincide with the 50th anniversary of the two General Election campaigns of 1974. The one in February 1974 was historic in that it produced five counts, the result was declared on the Friday evening and my majority was three.

So much has been written by Gwynfor and others that my recollection of the events of the time hopes to offer a balance or perhaps a correction to the accepted story. This account portrays the Gwynfor Evans and Plaid Cymru I was confronted with and remember back then.

There is little doubt that Gwynfor himself was

whitewashed by his followers to within a hair's breadth of a saint. But during my involvement with him, I didn't see a man who was anywhere near to being that. The impression I had was that he was a politician with weaknesses that had an adverse effect on his career.

I gave examples of why I believe this throughout this book, as I am not saying this lightly. Nor is it with any element of prejudice. This is the result of decades of evaluation, a man in his eighties doing what is described by Wordsworth as "emotions recollected in tranquility". Well, at least, as peaceful as politics in Wales can be! And I must note here also that I wasn't without my weaknesses either, and of course I made mistakes. Among them, so often a reluctance to seek advice from others before taking some key decisions; a tendency to be too outspoken; no time for politicians that waffled; seeing things in black and white with not allowing much room for shades of grey (a prerequisite to being a politician).

But the need to write this book wasn't only because of the involvement of the individuals with each other. I don't believe that there has ever been a period like the mid-Sixties and early Seventies in Welsh politics, the exact period of the battle between Gwynfor and myself. In this respect, we were lucky to be part of it. It was a period of battling and challenging the status quo, especially in constitutional matters relating to devolution and the status of the Welsh language. This is the period of Tryweryn, the Labour Party in 1964 winning an election for the first time since 1951, the days of violence, bombing, protesting and Cymdeithas yr Iaith and Saunders Lewis muddying the waters within Plaid Cymru.

This was also a period of animated debates about Europe and the serious divisions arising from that. This was when Britain joined the Common Market. Scarcely has there been a more bitter period, more inflammable, and with so much bickering in the history of Welsh politics. There is no doubt that this influenced Gwynfor and myself in our involvement with each other. The final chapter of this book will consider how much influence the bitterness of the period had on the way that Gwynfor and I responded to each other. Revisiting the story of Gwynfor and myself takes us back to an important period in our country's history. It was nothing like politics today.

In as much, the recording within these covers is a means of setting the politics of both Plaid Cymru and the Labour Party in the correct context for the period. How much did Plaid Cymru really achieve on devolution? – for example. What was the Labour Party's real stance on devolution? Gwynfor was very fond of claiming the praise for successes in the name of Plaid Cymru. He was much too ready to ignore what the Labour Party did in several areas, but specifically with regard to devolution, from the Fifties, through the Sixties and into the Seventies – I am thinking in particular of the contributions of Jim Griffiths, Cledwyn Hughes and John Morris. I'm saying all this as one who ultimately left the Labour Party.

That's the why, I'm sure. But what about the why now? There are many possible answers. Firstly, I effectively left politics in 1992, running a school inspection business. Undertaking inspections throughout Wales and England, employing over fifty people in two offices, meant that there was no time for politics of any sort.

But, in recent years, the political flame has rekindled, nudging me to becoming a public affairs commentator and observer with a blog, YouTube channel, Facebook page and Twitter (now X) account. I'm in my eighties and all are extremely active. So the old bug of the tendency to look back over my political years has returned again both with emotion and in time tranquility. The appetite is back.

But although the direct political involvement has waned, I kept all the archive material I had from the mid-sixties until 1974 and further. Therefore, my scrapbooks, full of newspaper cuttings, copies of speeches I made, books I published and also letters, have been a very valuable source for my research.

Another consideration that has reignited my desire to write this version of the book revolves around the current political situation. There is a similarity between several aspects of politics today and politics in the period of the book. Thankfully the hatred and violence have faded but the passion is still there. The leaders who followed Gwynfor didn't have to put up with the extremists from within and outside Plaid Cymru. But the issues are very similar. Discussing devolution and independence for Wales, for example, how do we grapple with the European question now Brexit has happened? Then what is to be the direction of travel both for Welsh Labour and Plaid Cymru? I'm sure that many things found in politics during the era of Gwynfor and myself will ring a bell with us today.

The final reason for writing this English version is a completely personal one. I have three children and six grandchildren. My children were young when I was politically active and a Member of Parliament, in fact my youngest Penri hadn't even been born. They certainly weren't old enough to understand the significance of my political work. This book is a means of putting what I did on record, for my children and grandchildren. It will be a means for them to understand and learn about my life when I was younger than my children are now. The three have made their own independent and successful ways in life. This is an opportunity for them to see how I did also.

Gwynoro Jones
June 2024

TWEETING, COLUMNS AND SCRAPBOOKS

This is the day and age when the former President of the United States several times a day communicates a substantial percentage of his statements on his social media platforms. We learn from the Covid Inquiry that the then British Prime Minister, his senior advisers and cabinet colleagues discussed views and opinions again daily via Whats App. Policy in a sentence that isn't on paper.

Gwynoro Jones's venture into political campaigning some fifty-eight years ago was a step into a completely different world. And I'm not talking about the colour of the politics either. Those were the days of weekly enthusiastic letters in local newspapers on local, national and international political issues. There were three in Gwynoro's constituency, the *Carmarthen Times*, the *Carmarthen Journal* and the South Wales *Guardian*, along with the *Western Mail* and the *Evening Post*. It wasn't just a couple of catchy lines by Mr or Mrs Dissatisfied from Cwmscwt. Many were half a page and more in papers that were substantial broadsheets. And there were numerous contributors.

But it wasn't only the public who would use the local newspapers to express their opinion on a bypass for Carmarthen, the price of milk, who owned Welsh water etc. This was where Gwynfor Evans and Gwynoro Jones themselves would air their opinions.

It could be argued that the current political discussion, although perhaps more often and regular, is less penetrating than it was in the days of the lengthy letters. Certainly, today's parliamentary candidates do not discuss their opinions on subjects in anywhere near as much detail as Gwynfor and Gwynoro did in their constituency's newspapers.

For me, the result of this was that I had a very rich source of information and opinions from the period, all in one important and valuable collection. There is one reason for this. Gwynoro Jones kept a stack of newspaper cuttings between 1966 and 1974. Indeed, he has a large number of scrapbooks full of cuttings that chronicle a substantial chunk of Welsh political history in such a troubled and key period as the end of the Sixties and early Seventies. Within these scrapbooks are hundreds of letters and articles by reporters and editors as well as those by Gwynoro and Gwynfor themselves. This is indeed an invaluable source of primary information for anyone who wants to write about the period, not only on Gwynoro Jones. The archive is currently being chronicled at the Welsh Political Archive Centre in Aberystwyth.

As a result, the research took a considerable amount of time. It is easier to read Twitter messages than yards of newspaper columns. But reading messages on social websites wouldn't have come close to creating the feeling, atmosphere and tension of the political battle in the history of Gwynoro and Gwynfor. Through the wad of printed records, one could really get to grips with the feelings and thoughts of members of the constituency, together with the way the two main political fighters got to grips with each other. It has been a valuable exercise, and in its own way, a completely historical one. Reading and analysing the scrapbooks gave a feeling of discussing and handling live historical documents, and that in a constituency which is unique in Welsh political history. It's a constituency that has provided several dramatic results throughout the years, and the battle between Gwynfor and Gwynoro is the most prominent.

Therefore, what you have in this volume is the fruit of reading editorial articles from the individual papers, letters from the residents of the Carmarthen constituency, articles by the members of both Gwynoro and Gwynfor's teams and substantial contributions by the two politicians themselves. In as much the writing process was reliant on three very valuable sources. The wad of newspaper cuttings kept by Gwynoro throughout the decades, the discussions and regular interviews with him over a period of a year or more and research in books relating to the period. The responses expressed at the time in the numerous letters and columns and Gwynoro's comments on the letters and subjects raised in them looking back over time.

The book relates the story as it was developing at the time. It is important and significant to remember this. Gwynoro also makes current comments as the story is told. Through this process, we get to know Gwynoro, the politician, as well as the person. And, of course, we come to know Gwynfor in the way that Gwynoro responds to him. This is Gwynoro's story, and therefore there isn't as much pressure to have Gwynfor's response to every point made by Gwynoro. Gwynoro would probably say that quite enough attention has been paid to Gwynfor's comments over the decades since 1974 and that it is now his turn! As a consequence, we hear several stories for the first time.

The book ends with Gwynoro weighing up his political career between 1966 and 1974 with the advantage of hindsight. With complete honesty, he weighs up the strengths and weaknesses of his political career. He acknowledges his failings. That in itself is a breath of fresh air in the current political climate. We have Gwynoro's interpretation of Gwynfor Evans's political contribution, one who was praised for his very authoritative and influential political status but, according to Gwynoro, was actually a man and not a saint with a number of weaknesses that were ignored by his followers. In telling his story, he argues his case.

Trying to understand two influential and independent political characters was a challenging experience, especially as one was alive and the other had died. But one thing is certain, it was an eye-opener for me, as one who remembers the hustle and bustle of the road sign and television channel protests of Cymdeithas yr Iaith, as well as the exciting elections of 1974. Without a doubt, in this volume, we have a glimpse of two prominent politicians in a period when Wales was on fire politically.

It has also, without a doubt, been a means of broadening my understanding of the political process. As one who remembers the nationalistic political scene of the Seventies, through the memory of a teenager at the time, it is too easy to think that discussing devolution began in 1979 with the referendum, and discussions to establish a Welsh Channel began in the early years of the Eighties. It is also easy to believe that all the developments in those areas came from one party, or one society alone. It was an eye-opener to see that the picture was much more complicated than that.

I'm sure Gwynoro and I don't agree on several political points. But, of course, that is not the point. Times have changed but perhaps things remain the same, and in the discussions that are tied in with the consequences of the withdrawal of Britain from the European Union, it is interesting to see the difference between the current Conservative Members of Parliament that hold one view but are voting the other way for the sake of their party, and Gwynoro sticking to his own principles even though doing so meant he stood against his own party. Conviction politics face to face with party politics.

My best wishes to anyone who will try and do similar work on the current era, relying on Twitter and Facebook messages as foundation sources. Thank goodness for local newspapers.

Alun Gibbard
March 2024

WHOSE WALES?: THE BATTLE FOR WELSH DEVOLUTION AND NATIONHOOD.
2021 – Gwynoro Jones and Alun Gibbard

Inside story of the setting up of the Royal Commission on the Constitution; Labour Wales evidence to it and Gwynfor Evans's discussions with the Heath government

The Home Secretary, Jim Callaghan, in the summer of 1968, proposed the idea of a constitutional commission. His aim was to see if any changes were needed to the functions of central government. By October, he reiterated that he thought that such a commission was the only answer as the government hadn't offered any credible alternative to the situation.

John Morris took the unusual step, in June 1968, of writing a memorandum to Prime Minister Harold Wilson, in order to give his thoughts on the Draft Conclusions of the Ministerial Committee on Devolution. Having reassured the Prime Minister that he had studied the document, he introduces his argument with this summary:

> *This is a sad document, not only for its conclusions, but worse, for its sheer argument on and lack of philosophy. There appear to be colleagues who do not wish to do anything, and others, who, when specific proposals are put, albeit on functions or decentralisation of administrative centres, if their own departments are affected, seek to reject them.*

Later that summer, in August, John Morris and Elystan Morgan discussed this constitutional situation while their families were on holiday together in Cornwall. John Morris recounts the story:

> *He told me, coming up from the beach one day, that he believed the answer to our problems was a Royal Commission for Wales and Scotland. It could consider whether any major changes were desirable for the fundamental reform of government. I immediately warmed to the suggestion, which was completely new to me.*

In his autobiography, *Atgofion Oes Elystan,* Lord Elystan Morgan recalls two meetings that have a significant role to play in this debate. He does not claim so himself; he never would. All he says is that in leaving both meetings, he felt satisfied that he had been true to his convictions. The first meeting was with Prime Minister Harold Wilson when Elystan had just been appointed as a Minister in the Home Office. He says that the meeting began with him re-iterating his belief in the need for Home Rule.

> *Even though there is clearly a very considerable feeling of disaffection towards the Government, I don't pretend to you that there is a pulsating power in Wales at the moment that represents a deep desire for a Parliament – I only wish there was. Plaid are being opportunistic and, like the Liberals in England, are exploiting a political vacuum.*

Wilson's response was to say that he realised that, but then asked Elystan Morgan what he should do in such a situation. The response outlined that the feelings of the people of Wales were far from insubstantial, even if there wasn't so much emphasis on a parliament for Wales. He emphasised that there was a layer of sincere patriotism on many levels in Wales that it would be foolish for the Labour Party to ignore.

> *If you give them the impression that you are totally intransigent, then that power may well rise against you. How exactly you do it is a matter for you – I can suggest two or three things, but I believe that a credible elected body for Wales is an absolute must.*

The second meeting was with Jim Callaghan, the Home Secretary. Elystan Morgan says that he was unaware that they had discussed the idea of a Commission prior to his meeting with Callaghan. He says that he outlined his arguments one by one and that Callaghan was particularly knowledgeable in his replies. The discussion had been ongoing for some time before Callaghan asked Elystan Morgan:

> *Well, what would you like to see?*
> *Policy A would be to block everything forever and pretend that Welsh nationhood does not exist – not my favoured option and one I believe that would be disastrous for the Labour Party, and unworthy of it, in light of its history. Yes, and your next point?*
> *The other extreme, of course, would be to plan immediately for a Welsh Home Rule Parliament, if not for Welsh independence. A middle course would be to show imagina-*

tion, progressiveness and understanding of Welsh nation-
hood that would carry with you the majority of opinion in
Wales and Scotland, and possibly in England as well. That
would be the course that I would counsel.

Oh, and how do you achieve that?

By setting up a Royal Commission to study that question.

By the October of that year, Callaghan had said that he saw no alternative to establishing a commission, as the government had not come up with an alternative and that the administrative and parliamentary devolution that had been discussed were insufficient by themselves. In his memoirs, John Morris reflects on this move:

In my view, it could act as a catalyst for fundamental con-
stitutional changes for Wales that we could hardly dream
of. If the evidence went well, there could be immense
changes. Looking back onto my interest and discussions in
the early 1950s, we were now in a new field – or perhaps
better expressed, on a 'new planet'... Here, to me, was a
practical way forward with immense potential.

He is clearly enthused by such a prospect. Not all were, of course. As we have seen, Morris himself had commented on the effect of Plaid Cymru gains between 1966 and 1968, calling them a "looming danger". Critics of a constitutional commission saw that calling for such an enquiry was a reaction to nationalist success. But Morris rejected this:

So it might appear. To me, it was different.

Prime Minister Harold Wilson announced the forming of
the Commission in October 1968, led by Lord Crowther.
He died soon after, and Lord Kilbrandon took his place.

This is when the devolution issue became an active part
of my political life. It landed on my plate with a vengeance
when I was asked to chair a working party to prepare the
Labour Party's evidence to the Kilbrandon Commission.
It was also the time I met up with the key people in the
party in London – Sir Harry Nicholas, Gwyn Morgan, Ron
Hayward and Margaret Jackson (later Beckett).

We were a team of seven and we worked exceptionally
diligently for months. It was an interesting group – Paul
Flynn, Alun Michael, the lecturer and broadcaster Barry
Jones. Bruce George, who at the time was a farmer near
Monmouth and eventually became a West Midlands MP,
Wyn Thomas much later of Swansea Sound fame and
Gareth Howell who was the son of Lyn Howell of the
Wales Tourist Board.

There were monthly reports to the Welsh Executive and a
few meetings with the Welsh Labour group of MPs. Most of
them were heated discussions and I remember George
Thomas and the South Wales Valley MPs getting very
animated and hostile. The reality was that the party in Wales
just did not wish to go down this road. But there were good
allies on the executive, Jack Brooks being one, and since he
was Callaghan's agent, I got the sense of what the then
Labour government was expecting from our evidence.
However, the records will show that the group recommended
an all-Wales body much stronger than the actual evidence
presented to the Kilbrandon Commission and included in its
report when it was published in October 1973.

The group was in favour of a legislative body, but opposition was strong in both the Welsh Labour executive and the Welsh Labour Group of MPs. The final report Reform of the Machinery of Government was presented to the Welsh Executive and MPs in August 1969.

The general principle was that those powers residing in the Welsh Office at the time and those of Welsh departments within other ministries should become the responsibility of an elected Welsh Council, which would have 72 members for a fixed term of four years.

They also proposed shared responsibility between the Council and Westminster – on economic planning and industrial development, social security, water resources and agriculture, for example. It was suggested that a Joint Committee should be established with Westminster on future devolution operations.

While Prime Minister Harold Wilson was on his holidays in 1969, in his favourite Scilly Isles, he received a letter from George Thomas, who wanted to outline his thoughts on increased powers for Wales. As John Morris says:

George was seeking to exploit what was understood to be his special relationship with the Prime Minister. He certainly believed that he had such a relationship.

George Thomas called for an elected, or partly elected, Welsh Council, with members being paid.

The functions of the Welsh Council could be partly executive and partly advisory. The following responsibilities are amongst those that could be administered by the council,

*namely: the Health services in Wales, the Welsh Arts
Council, the Welsh Committee of the Forestry Commission,
The Welsh Committee of the Countryside Commission, the
Welsh Joint Education Committee, the present advisory re-
sponsibilities of the current nominated Welsh Council, the
Welsh Committee of the Water Resources Board, the Central
Training Council (Welsh Committee), the Youth Employment
Council (Welsh Committee).*

He ends his letter to the Prime Minister calling for administrative devolution, not parliamentary devolution.

With Gwynfor Evans in Westminster by now, he was,
of course, able to have discussions with Ministers and
MPs he otherwise wouldn't have been able to have.
There's a record of meetings he had in 1968 in Plaid
Cymru's Executive Committee's minutes. They were
meetings he had with the Conservative Party. He had
several meetings with Willie Whitelaw, the Tory Chief
Whip, and Keith Joseph, who, in the previous government,
was Minister for Housing and Local Government. A copy
of the memo written to summarise one of the meetings
between Gwynfor and Willie Whitelaw is included with
Plaid's minutes and marked Completely Confidential.

*Three significant points have emerged from the Evans/
Whitelaw meeting.*
*a. Whitelaw states his opinion that Wales and Scotland are
nations in a sense that England is not.*
*b. Gwynfor Evans emphasised that it is essential for the
London Government to manifest some response to
political and constitutional nationalist activity if the con-*

217

clusion that Westminster will only respond to unconstitutional or violent action is to be avoided. The failure of Westminster to respond to political and constitutional pressure in the case of Tryweryn – and much earlier, the failure to respond to constitutional demands by Irish nationalists in 1912 (which would not have led to the violence of 1916/22) was discussed. Whitelaw conceded that authority must respond to political pressure as well as to violence.

c. *Whitelaw did not see the English consenting to Plaid Cymru's demands in toto, although he conceded the reasonableness of our British Common Market Policy. Gwynfor Evans related how he found MPs on both sides of the House accepting that if the people of Wales wanted full self-government, then they should be given it. Granted that Plaid Cymru would accept nothing less than its ultimate goal, Whitelaw enquired whether an elected Council for Wales would be acceptable as an interim measure. Gwynfor Evans said that the opportunity for such a development had been lost by the Labour Government and nothing short of a Parliament would now be acceptable (as a 'step in the right direction'). A discussion followed on the nature of such a Parliament.*

The memo confirms that a meeting with Mr Heath, party leader Edward Heath, is in the offing. The minutes end in this way:

Conclusion: Mr Gwynfor Evans is of the opinion that the Tories are now willing to think seriously in terms of a Welsh Parliament.

This was when the Tories were still saying they were
opposed to a Secretary of State for Wales. It's another
example of Gwynfor's dreaming – that's the only way he
could have gone from the discussions outlined in the
memo to concluding that the Tories were now thinking of
a Parliament for Wales.

Modern Wales by Parthian Books

The Modern Wales Series, edited by Dai Smith and supported by the Rhys Davies Trust, was launched in 2017. The Series offers an extensive list of biography, memoir, history and politics which reflect and analyse the development of Wales as a modernised society into contemporary times. It engages widely across places and people, encompasses imagery and the construction of iconography, dissects historiography and recounts plain stories, all in order to elucidate the kaleidoscopic pattern which has shaped and changed the complex culture and society of Wales and the Welsh.

The inaugural titles in the Series were *To Hear the Skylark's Song*, a haunting memoir of growing up in Aberfan by Huw Lewis, and Joe England's panoramic *Merthyr: The Crucible of Modern Wales*. The impressive list has continued with Angela John's *Rocking the Boat*, essays on Welsh women who pioneered the universal fight for equality and Daryl Leeworthy's landmark overview *Labour Country*, on the struggle through radical action and social democratic politics to ground Wales in the civics of common ownership. Myths and misapprehension, whether naïve or calculated, have been ruthlessly filleted in Martin Johnes's startling *Wales: England's Colony?* and a clutch of biographical studies will reintroduce us to the once seminal, now neglected, figures of Cyril Lakin, Minnie Pallister and Gwyn Thomas, whilst Meic Stephens's *Rhys Davies: A Writer's Life* and Dai Smith's *Raymond Williams: A Warrior's Tale* form part of an associated back catalogue from Parthian.

the RHYS DAVIES TRUST

PARTHIAN

MODERN WALES

WALES: ENGLAND'S COLONY?

Martin Johnes

From the very beginnings of Wales, its people have defined themselves against their large neighbour. This book tells the fascinating story of an uneasy and unequal relationship between two nations living side-by-side.

PB / £8.99
978-1-912681-41-9

RHYS DAVIES: A WRITER'S LIFE

Meic Stephens

Rhys Davies (1901-78) was among the most dedicated, prolific and accomplished of Welsh prose writers. This is his first full biography.

'This is a delightful book, which is itself a social history in its own right, and funny.'
– The Spectator

PB / £11.99
978-1-912109-96-8

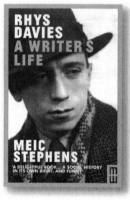

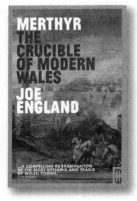

MERTHYR, THE CRUCIBLE OF MODERN WALES

Joe England

Merthyr Tydfil was the town where the future of a country was forged: a thriving, struggling surge of people, industry, democracy and ideas. This book assesses an epic history of Merthyr from 1760 to 1912 through the focus of a fresh and thoroughly convincing perspective.

PB / £18.99
978-1-913640-05-7

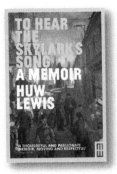

TO HEAR THE SKYLARK'S SONG

Huw Lewis

To Hear the Skylark's Song is a memoir about how Aberfan survived and eventually thrived after the terrible disaster of the 21st of October 1966.

'A thoughtful and passionate memoir, moving and respectful.'
– Tessa Hadley

PB / £8.99
978-1-912109-72-2

ROCKING THE BOAT

Angela V. John

This insightful and revealing collection of essays focuses on seven Welsh women who, in a range of imaginative ways, resisted the status quo in Wales, England and beyond during the nineteenth and twentieth centuries.

PB / £11.99
978-1-912681-44-0

TURNING THE TIDE

Angela V. John

This rich biography tells the remarkable tale of Margaret Haig Thomas (1883-1958) who became the second Viscountess Rhondda. She was a Welsh suffragette, held important posts during the First World War and survived the sinking of the *Lusitania*.

PB / £17.99
978-1-909844-72-8

BRENDA CHAMBERLAIN, ARTIST & WRITER

Jill Piercy

The first full-length biography of Brenda Chamberlain chronicles the life of an artist and writer whose work was strongly affected by the places she lived, most famously Bardsey Island and the Greek island of Hydra.

PB / £11.99
978-1-912681-06-8

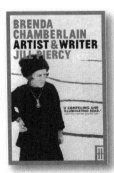

PARTHIAN

 MODERN WALES

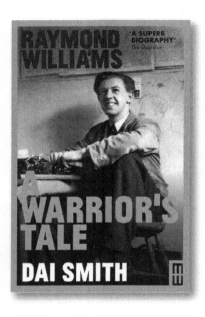

RAYMOND WILLIAMS: A WARRIOR'S TALE

Dai Smith

Raymond Williams (1921-1998) was the most influential socialist writer and thinker in post-war Britain. Now, for the first time, making use of Williams's private and unpublished papers and by placing him in a wide social and cultural landscape, Dai Smith, in this highly original and much praised biography, uncovers how Williams's life to 1961 is an explanation of his immense intellectual achievement.

'Becomes at once the authoritative account... Smith has done all that we can ask the historian as biographer to do.'
– Stefan Collini, *London Review of Books*

PB / £16.99
978-1-913640-08-8

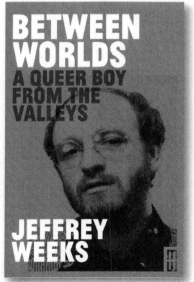

BETWEEN WORLDS: A QUEER BOY FROM THE VALLEYS

Jeffrey Weeks

A man's own story from the Rhondda. Jeffrey Weeks was born in the Rhondda in 1945, of mining stock. As he grew up he increasingly felt an outsider in the intensely community-minded valleys, a feeling intensified as he became aware of his gayness. Escape came through education. He left for London, to university, and to realise his sexuality. He has been described as the 'most significant British intellectual working on sexuality to emerge from the radical sexual movements of the 1970s'.

HB / £20
978-1-912681-88-4

I Gwynoro Jones
Aelod Seneddol dros Gaerfyrddin 1970 – 1974

Mae'n wir nad oeddem o'r un blaid wleidyddol;
Ond rhydd yw i bob dyn ei gred ai farn
Crwydraist yn eiddgar dros y llawr seneddol
Gan chwalu'r hen ragfarnau i gyd yn sarn:
Collaist ddafnau o chwys yn ol dy gredo
A throi pob carreg dros yr hyn oedd iawn
Deliaist ati'n weithgar heb laesu dwylo
Gan gyflawni dy ddiwrnod gwaith yn llawn,
Marchogaist fel Yntau ar ebol asyn
A'r dorf yn taenu llawryf dan dy draed,
Canwyd dy glodydd yn ddiddiwedd wedyn
Er bod 'na rywrai'n ysu am dy waed,
A chroeshoeliwyd di gan yr un hen griw
A floeddiai "Hosanna!" ar ffordd Jeriw

D.H. Culpitt 1976

Still Campaigning Carmarthen June 2024.

To achieve a Sovereign Wales will undoubtedly require even more determined and relentless campaigning.

Making a brief contribution in AUOB rally in Carmarthen is an honour and not only will it be a source of memories past but to impress on a much younger audience to hold firm to the faith; as post General Election Wales will face many challenges over its future governance but there also will be significant opportunities too as the years unfold. Building a structure and developing a roadmap that will lead to a Sovereign Wales is now essential. Engaging with the people on a wider forum than rallies.

Probably terms like "freedom", "self-governing Wales", "free Wales" are more appealing to the mass of our people than the word "independence" which has carried for decades an association with a "separate Wales".

We have gone through a five-year period where the future of Wales has been talked about ad nauseum. There are more than sufficient articles, podcasts, videos, campaign rallies, Blogs, booklets, books and even Commission reports available for public consumption. In essence there is no more to be written or said on the various options to be considered over the future governance of Wales. What is urgently required now is ACTION.

It's time to set up something akin to citizen assemblies and most importantly establish a Wales Standing Convention to move forward. Bringing together representatives from civic society, local government, trade unions, academic institutions, voluntary and charitable organisations, and political organisations.

Question is, do we have the will to do this?

Gwynoro Jones, June 2024